MOON

- BEST OF -

GRAND CANYON

Tim Hull

GRAND CANYON NATIONAL PARK

To Las Vegas

Paiute Wilderness Area

Grand Wash

Grand Wash Cliffs Wilderness Area

Grand Canyon-Parashant National Monument

Parashant Creek

Mount Trumbull Wilderness Area

Tuweep

Mount Logan Wilderness Area

Toroweap Point

TOROWEAP OVERLOOK

Lake Mead National Recreation Area

Mohawk Creek

Grand Canyon West

GRAND CANYON SKYWALK

Grand Canyon National Park

Colorado River

INDIAN ROUTE 18

Hualapai Reservation

DIAMOND CREEK RD

BUCK AND DOE ROAD

HISTORIC ROUTE 66

HUALAPAI RIVER RUNNERS

Peach Springs

66

0   8 mi

0   8 km

Scenic Drive

Inset map

NEVADA

UTAH

St George

Page

MAP AREA

Las Vegas

Lake Mead

Grand Canyon National Park

89

160

CALIFORNIA

Grand Canyon Village

Cameron

93

Peach Springs

Bullhead City

Seligman

Kingman

Williams

Flagstaff

40

Sedona

93

17

60

60

10

PHOENIX

0   50 mi

0   50 km

© MOON.COM

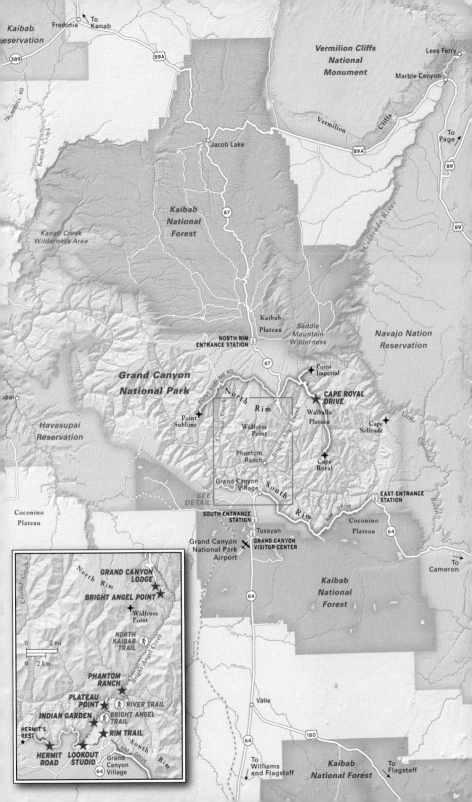

CONTENTS

14

35

87

143

161

184

Although every effort was made to make sure the information in this book was accurate when going to press, research was impacted by the COVID-19 pandemic and things may have changed since the time of writing. Be sure to confirm specific details, like opening hours, closures, and travel guidelines and restrictions, when making your travel plans. For more detailed information, see page 222.

Grand Canyon National Park

WELCOME TO
GRAND
CANYON

Speaking from the South Rim of the Grand Canyon in 1903, President Theodore Roosevelt declared, "Leave it as it is. You cannot improve on it; not a bit." Even today, the canyon simply must be seen to be believed. If you stand for the first time on one of the South Rim's easily accessible lookouts and don't need to catch your breath, you might need to check your pulse. The canyon is a water-wrought cathedral, a deep rock labyrinth whose layers of primordial earth tell the history of the planet. Take your time simply staring into its brash vastness—you'll need it.

The more adventurous can make reservations, obtain a permit, and enter the desert depths of the canyon, taking a hike, or even a mule ride, to the Colorado River or spending a weekend trekking rim to rim with an overnight at the famous Phantom Ranch, deep in the canyon's inner gorge. The really brave can hire a guide and take a once-in-a-lifetime trip down the great river, riding the roiling rapids and camping on its serene beaches.

There are plenty of places to stay and eat, many of them charming and historic, on the canyon's South Rim. If you decide to go to the high, forested, and often snowy North Rim, you'll drive through a corner of the desolate Arizona Strip and onto the Kaibab Plateau, which have a beauty and a history all their own.

South Kaibab Trail

BEST DAY IN
GRAND
CANYON

Morning

1 If you only have a day at the Grand Canyon, you'd be wise to spend it on the South Rim, especially if it's your first trip here. Start early at the Grand Canyon Visitor Center, watching the 20-minute movie about the canyon. From the visitor center, walk out to **Mather Point** for your first breathtaking view of the canyon. *page 41*

2 Walk the Rim Trail (or ride the free shuttle bus) to **Yavapai Geology Museum** (0.8 mi/1.3 km), the best place in the park to learn about canyon geology. *page 41*

Afternoon

3 Continue on the Rim Trail (or shuttle) to **Grand Canyon Village** (1.5 mi/2.4 km), stopping to look at the romantic architecture, peruse the gift shops, and watch California condors soaring over the canyon. Eat lunch at one of the restaurants in the village. *page 44*

4 Fueled up for your second act, cycle or walk the Rim Trail (or take the free shuttle bus) along the 14-mile (22.5-km) round-trip **Hermit Road;** spend 2-3 hours stopping at all the viewpoints from Maricopa Point to Hermit's Rest, then stop by your room or campsite for a rest and refresh before evening arrives. *page 49*

Evening

5 Start watching the sunset from **Yavapai Point** (where the Yavapai Geology Museum is located). *page 44*

6 Stroll along the canyon rim as the sun smolders and sinks, ending at **El Tovar** (1 mi/1.6 km from Yavapai Point) for dinner (reservation required). Afterward, attend a free ranger talk (held at 8:30pm daily) on the Grand Canyon's natural and human history at McKee Amphitheater. *page 66*

ITINERARY DETAILS

- The park's free **shuttles** run year-round.

- **Hermit Road** is open to private vehicles November-March, a less crowded time of year when you can drive to the viewpoints instead of taking the shuttle. (May-Oct. only free shuttles and bikes are allowed on Hermit Road, while both shuttles and private cars drive Hermit Road Nov.-Mar.)

- Rent bikes at **Bright Angel Bicycles** near the visitor center, or bring your own.

- Summer, spring, and early fall (the busiest seasons at Grand Canyon National Park) make dinner reservations at **El Tovar** (tel. 928/638-2631, ext. 6432; www.grandcanyonlodges.com) far in advance.

- Depending on the season of your visit, **sunset** might happen before or after dinner. In summer, sunset lasts until around 8 or 8:30pm; in fall and winter, sunset ends around 6:30-7pm. Fortunately, **El Tovar** is open until 9pm for dining and until 10pm in the lounge year-round.

- Free **ranger talks** are popular and may require advance tickets, available starting at 7:30pm at the Shrine of the Ages venue near Park Headquarters. If the weather isn't nice, Shrine of Ages also serves as an alternate venue for the talk.

pine along the South Rim

SEASONS OF THE GRAND CANYON

SUMMER
(MAY-AUG., HIGH SEASON)

The high season on the park's **South and North Rims** comes in summer. Expect crowds at the most popular viewpoints and sights along the South Rim; lines at the main South Entrance and the shuttle bus stops; full lodges, campgrounds, and eateries; and busloads of tourists from around the globe. But with pleasant daytime temperatures, the crowds can hardly spoil a day spent walking along the Rim Trail and exploring Grand Canyon Village.

Inside the Grand Canyon, temperatures regularly exceed 110°F (43°C) during the hottest part of the day, when all creatures within the gorge seek their hidden recesses of shade. The area is pleasant and safe only in the early morning and evening.

Late-afternoon thunderstorms, often with spectacular displays of lightning, are a common occurrence throughout the region from July-September.

Temperatures

South and North Rims: Averaging 70s (21 to 26°C) and 80s (27 to 32°C) during the day, and 50s (10 to 15°C) and 60s (16 to 21°C) at night.
Inner Canyon: Highs of 110°F (43°C) during the day, and lows in the 60s-70s F (16 to 26°C) at night.

SPRING AND FALL
(MID-MAR.-APR. AND SEPT.-OCT., MID-SEASON)

Spring and fall are still busy but with

summer rainstorm over Grand Canyon

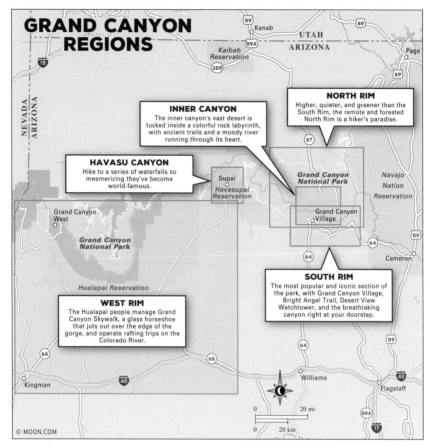

GRAND CANYON REGIONS

INNER CANYON
The inner canyon's vast desert is tucked inside a colorful rock labyrinth, with ancient trails and a moody river running through its heart.

NORTH RIM
Higher, quieter, and greener than the South Rim, the remote and forested North Rim is a hiker's paradise.

HAVASU CANYON
Hike to a series of waterfalls so mesmerizing they've become world-famous.

SOUTH RIM
The most popular and iconic section of the park, with Grand Canyon Village, Bright Angel Trail, Desert View Watchtower, and the breathtaking canyon right at your doorstep.

WEST RIM
The Hualapai people manage Grand Canyon Skywalk, a glass horseshoe that juts out over the edge of the gorge, and operate rafting trips on the Colorado River.

UTAH
ARIZONA
Kanab
Page
Kaibab Reservation
NEVADA / ARIZONA
Grand Canyon West
Grand Canyon National Park
Hualapai Reservation
Supai
Havasupai Reservation
Grand Canyon National Park
Grand Canyon Village
Navajo Nation Reservation
Cameron
Williams
Kingman
Flagstaff

0   20 mi
0   20 km

© MOON.COM

---

cooler temps in the inner canyon. Mid-season offers something of the best of both worlds—**pleasant (though often windy) days and cool nights on the rims** and **near-ideal conditions for backpacking** and exploring inside the canyon. Backcountry permits and river-trip reservations are, as a result, more difficult to obtain during the mid-season months. Inside the canyon, spring starts in early March and fall stretches into November.

Temperatures

South and North Rims: Averaging 60s-80s (27 to 32°C) during the day, and 30s (4 to 9°C) to 50s (10 to 15°C) at night.

Inner Canyon: Highs in 80s-100s (27 to 41°C) during the day, and lows in the 50s-70s (10 to 26°C) at night.

WINTER
(NOV.-MID-MAR., LOW SEASON)

The remote **North Rim closes for the season** by early November, with the Kaibab Plateau blanketed in snow. On the **South Rim,** there is usually an early-winter rush, but by January it has entered its relatively slow low season, which lasts through about mid-March when the first of the spring break crowds arrive. Though cold and periodically snowy, the low

NEED TO KNOW

- **Park website:** www.nps.gov/grca
- **Entrance fee:** $35 per vehicle per park
- **Main entrance:** South Entrance (AZ 64)
- **Main visitor center:** Grand Canyon Visitor Center (near Mather Point)
- **Hotel and park activity reservations:**
  - **Xanterra:** www.grandcanyonlodges.com
  - **Delaware North:** www.visitgrandcanyon.com
- **Campsite reservations:** recreation.gov
- **Grand Canyon West reservations:** www.grandcanyonwest.com
- **Havasupai reservations:** www.havasupaireservations.com
- **Gas in the park:** Desert View, North Rim Campground
- **High season:** May-August

season is a great time to be at the South Rim. A light but warm coat, a wool hat, and a pair of gloves are all you need to enjoy a winter visit to the canyon. You may find significant discounts on accommodations throughout the region during this season, but also curtailed services.

On a **winter backpacking** trip into the **inner canyon** from the South Rim, you'll encounter cool days, cold nights, and fewer people (permit required).

Temperatures

South and North Rims: Averaging in the 40s and 50s (4 to 9°C) during the day, and 20s (-7 to -15°C) and teens (-12 to -7°C) at night.

Inner Canyon: Highs in the 40s and 50s (4 to 9°C) during the day, and lows in the 30s and 40s (-1 to 9°C) at night. (Cold air gets trapped in the canyon, cooling it down to temperatures similar to that on the rims in winter.)

Closures

The **North Rim** is typically closed November-mid-May, with the only road leading to the area, **AZ 67,** closed December-mid-May. Commercial river trips through the inner canyon do not run during winter (rafting season runs Apr.-Oct.).

view from Lookout Studio

BEST OF THE BEST
GRAND
CANYON

BEST HIKES

RIM TRAIL: BRIGHT ANGEL LODGE TO MATHER POINT
South Rim
EASY

Heading east from Bright Angel Lodge along the South Rim's paved and generally level Rim Trail, this 2.5-mile (4-km) one-way hike passes the historic lodges and shops at Grand Canyon Village, the Trail of Time, and Yavapai Geology Museum on the way to Mather Point—with the Grand Canyon spreading out on your left side the whole way. If you don't feel like walking back, hop on a shuttle bus nearby (page 60).

BRIGHT ANGEL TRAIL
South Rim
MODERATE TO STRENUOUS

Introduce yourself to the inner canyon on a 3-mile (4.8-km) round-trip hike from the South Rim down the steep and twisting Bright Angel Trail, passing through a rock tunnel

and ending at a resthouse along the trail, where you'll turn around and start your (eventually) rewarding climb back out (page 58).

NORTH KAIBAB TRAIL
North Rim
MODERATE TO VERY STRENUOUS

Step aside for the mule trains on this hike into Grand Canyon from the North Rim. If you turn around at Supai Tunnel, which was blasted into the rock walls along the trail, this makes for a 4-mile (6.4-km) round-trip hike (page 102).

WIDFORSS TRAIL
North Rim
EASY TO MODERATE

Get to know the forests of the North Rim on this 10-mile (16.1-km) round-trip hike among pines, firs, and aspens to Widforss Point, a spectacular viewpoint named for the beloved Grand Canyon artist Gunnar Widforss (page 104).

RIVER TRAIL
Inner Canyon
EASY

Look for bighorn sheep as you traverse the Colorado River deep in the Inner Canyon on this 1.5-mile (2.4-km) loop (page 140).

River Trail

Bright Angel Trail

Grandview Point

BEST VIEWS

LOOKOUT STUDIO
South Rim

A Mary Colter-designed stone building hanging off the rim in Grand Canyon Village, Lookout Studio's multi-level porches and verandas provide breathtaking views of Grand Canyon and a chance to see California condors soaring overhead (page 47).

HOPI POINT
South Rim

Probably the most recommended spot on the South Rim for viewing the sunset, Hopi Point has wide and long views of the canyon and a fun, convivial atmosphere most nights, as travelers from around the world gather together to watch and photograph the performance (page 49).

GRANDVIEW POINT
South Rim

Hopi guides brought Spanish explorers near this now-legendary viewpoint along Desert View Drive to show them the Grand Canyon for the first time. The vista features sweeping views of the western and eastern canyons and also peeks at the Colorado River, Desert View Watchtower, and the North Rim (page 51).

BRIGHT ANGEL POINT
North Rim

The North Rim's primary viewpoint, Bright Angel Point juts out into Bright Angel Canyon at the end of a 0.3-mile (0.5-km) walk on a paved trail behind Grand Canyon Lodge. Here, the convergence of three tributary canyons—Roaring Springs, Transept, and Bright Angel—creates a vast and thrilling labyrinth (page 89).

CAPE ROYAL
North Rim

Cape Royal, a jutting rock platform hovering over the gorge among looming rock temples and monuments, waits to be discovered at the end of a long forest drive along the rim (page 98).

Lookout Studio (left); Bright Angel Point (right)

INDIGENOUS PEOPLES OF THE GRAND CANYON

Humans have lived in the Grand Canyon for at least 12,000 years. All along the Colorado River through the canyon, archeologists have found masonry rooms, hearths, roasting pits, tools, pottery, and other evidence of ancient cultures, including ruins of small, seasonally occupied pueblos on both the South and North Rims. Ancient hunter-gatherers first occupied Grand Canyon about 9,000-12,000 years ago, and later Archaic People (2,500-9,000 years ago) left behind mysterious "split-twig figurines," small, probably ceremonial, animal effigies made from splitting and twisting willow switches. Around 200 of these figurines have been found in caves and elsewhere in the canyon. When the Basketmaker culture moved into the canyon region about 1,200-2,500 years ago, it brought pit houses, the bow and arrow, and agriculture. By AD 800-1300, the Ancestral Puebloans, the ancestors of the Hopi, Zuni, and other Pueblo tribes of the Southwest, were building masonry architecture on both rims and along the river, and growing corn, beans, and squash to support relatively populous communities. Between 1300-1500, the ancestors of several canyon-country Native American tribes moved into the region, including the forebears of the Navajo, the Hualapai, the Havasupai, and the Southern Paiute.

LEGACY

Native American tribes traditionally linked to the Grand Canyon—the **Hopi, Navajo, Yavapai-Apache,**

Walhalla Glades Pueblo

Havasupai, Hualapai, and **Southern Paiute**—live and thrive in the region today. The **Navajo Nation** and
the **Hopi Mesas** are just to the east
of Grand Canyon National Park,
the **Hualapai Tribe** operates Grand
Canyon West and the Skywalk on
their land in the western canyon,
the **Havasupai** live in the village of
Supai, deep within the western canyon, and the **Southern Paiute** live
near the North Rim and in Southern
Utah. Many tribal members continue to foster a sacred bond with this
mysterious and spiritual landscape,
collecting traditional plants, min-
erals, and other materials from the
canyon.

EXPERIENCES

There are many ways for visitors
to engage with Indigenous communities and cultures with deep
ties to Grand Canyon country. In
addition to the experiences listed
below, the park hosts Native American heritage events, talks, and art
demonstrations throughout the
year. Check the park's calendar of
events for details. For authentic Native American arts and crafts check
out **Hopi House** (page 45) and
the **El Tovar gift shop** (page 72),
where you can purchase heirlooms
and support local Indigenous artists
at the same time.

Tusayan Ruin & Museum

On the South Rim, drive 22 miles
(35.4 km) east of Grand Canyon
Village along Desert View Drive to
explore an 800-year-old Ancestral
Puebloan ruin via a self-guided
trail, and peruse a small museum
collection of canyonland Native
American artifacts (page 51).

Walhalla Glades Pueblo and Cliff Spring Trail

On the North Rim, drive 18 miles
(30 km) along the Cape Royal
Road to Walhalla Glades Pueblo
(page 90), the ruins of a small
settlement occupied from around
AD 1050-1150. Just up the road, hike
the easy 1-mile (1.6-km) round-
trip Cliff Spring Trail to a granary
built by Ancestral Puebloans (page
104). In the canyon below this
area is the Unkar Delta, which from
around AD 850-1200 was occupied
and farmed by the same people
who built the rim-top pueblo.

Hike to Havasu Canyon

Secure a reservation and a permit
to hike the 8-mile (12.9-km) one-
way trail to Supai, a small village
inside the western Grand Canyon
where the Havasupai have lived for
centuries. The lush and beautiful riparian area is world-famous for its
blue-green waterfalls (page 186).

West Rim

In the early 2000s, the Hualapai
Nation partnered with Las Vegas
entrepreneur David Jin and built
The Skywalk, a 70-foot-long (21-
m) glass walkway hanging from
the Grand Canyon's western rim,
transforming the once empty and
lonely corner of Grand Canyon into
a thriving tourist enterprise focused
on tours from Las Vegas (page
166). The **Hualapai River Runners**,
based out of nearby Peach Springs,
will take you on a one-day river trip
on the mighty Colorado River (page
172).

BEST ARCHITECTURE

In the 1920s and 1930s, the Fred Harvey Company (the main concessionaire of the Santa Fe Railroad, which was responsible for the tourism boom in the canyon) enlisted Arts and Crafts designer and architect **Mary Jane Colter** to build lodges, lookouts, galleries, and stores on the South Rim. Colter's interest in and understanding of Ancestral Puebloan and Puebloan architecture and lifeways infused her designs. These treasured buildings still stand today, and are now considered to be some of the finest architectural accomplishments in the entire national parks system.

DESERT VIEW WATCHTOWER
South Rim

Colter's elegant stone tower overlooking the eastern canyon's desert is meant to echo ancient Ancestral Puebloan structures in the Four Corners region. Hopi artist Frank Kabotie painted its rounded walls with images from Hopi religion and lore (page 53).

HERMIT'S REST
South Rim

Colter also designed this stone-and-timber resthouse and giftshop on the far western edge of the park, at the end of the Hermit Road. The cramped entrance releases into a high-ceilinged great room with hanging metal lanterns, dominated by a stone hearth with rustic handmade chairs and a huge fireplace (page 50).

EL TOVAR
South Rim

Designed by Charles Whittlesey and built by the Santa Fe Railroad in 1905, this legendary hotel, formerly managed by the Fred Harvey Company, looks a bit like a European hunting lodge perched on the rim of a vast

Desert View Watchtower (top); El Tovar (bottom)

PRACTICING SUSTAINABLE TRAVEL IN GRAND CANYON

- Bring reusable water bottles and refill them at water stations across the park.
- Park the car as soon as you arrive, and walk, bike, or ride the free shuttle buses for the rest of your stay.
- Stay at in-park lodges or campgrounds to reduce driving.
- Leave your car outside the park, and bike the 6.5-mile (10.5-km) Tusayan Greenway to the park.
- Follow basic Leave No Trace principles (https://lnt.org/why/7-principles).

desert canyon. Visited by princes, presidents, and movie stars, El Tovar was the first great hotel on the rim, and it remains so today. The dining room is also a standout (page 72).

GRAND CANYON LODGE
North Rim

This native-stone-and-log lodge opened in 1937 on the very edge of the Grand Canyon's forested North Rim, featuring a sunroom with huge picture windows framing the canyon, a long veranda, and a

soaring window-lined dining room (page 114).

GRAND CANYON SKYWALK
West Rim

Opened to the public in 2007 and operated by the Hualapai Tribe, the Skywalk is the futuristic counterpart to Colter's South Rim structures. Step out onto this glass horseshoe that dangles over the canyon, and—if you're brave enough—stare straight down into the canyon's depths (page 166).

BEST SCENIC DRIVE

CAPE ROYAL DRIVE

PARK AREA: North Rim
SEASON: Late May-mid-October
DRIVING DISTANCE: 23 miles
(37 km) one-way, plus 3-mile (4.8-km)
one-way side trip
DRIVING TIME: 2 hours one-way
(plus 30-40-minute side trip)

This stunning drive skirts the highland forest of the North Rim, ending at Cape Royal with views of the Colorado River and the South Rim across the canyon. Along the way are several developed viewpoints with parking, each of which provides a different perspective on the canyon. Highlights include **Point Imperial,** a slight detour that provides a southeast-facing view of the white-rock peak **Mount Hayden** and across the red-and-green canyon to the Painted Desert on Navajoland; **Vista Encantada** ("enchanting view"), which has a gorgeous view and is a great spot for a picnic; and the terminus at **Cape Royal,** which is reached by an easy, paved trail (about 1 mi/1.6 km round-trip). Along the trail you'll pass the rock arch **Angels Window,** which offers a perfectly framed view of the river (page 95).

Cape Royal

CAPE ROYAL DRIVE

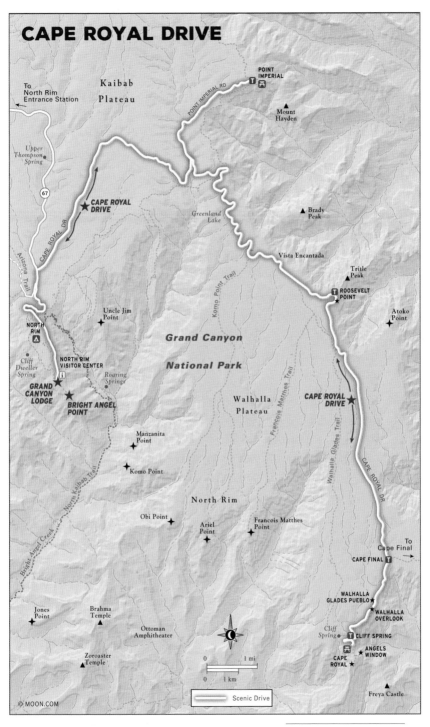

To North Rim Entrance Station

Kaibab Plateau

POINT IMPERIAL

POINT IMPERIAL RD

Mount Hayden

Upper Thompson Spring

67

CAPE ROYAL DRIVE

Greenland Lake

Brady Peak

Arizona Trail

Vista Encantada

Tritle Peak

ROOSEVELT POINT

Atoko Point

Uncle Jim Point

Komo Point Trail

Grand Canyon

National Park

NORTH RIM

CAPE ROYAL DRIVE

Cliff Dweller Spring

NORTH RIM VISITOR CENTER

Roaring Springs

GRAND CANYON LODGE

BRIGHT ANGEL POINT

Walhalla Plateau

Francois Matthes Trail

CAPE ROYAL DR

North Kaibab Trail

Manzanita Point

Komo Point

Walhalla Glades Trail

North Rim

Obi Point

Ariel Point

Francois Matthes Point

To Cape Final

Bright Angel Creek

CAPE FINAL

WALHALLA GLADES PUEBLO

Jones Point

Brahma Temple

Ottoman Amphitheater

WALHALLA OVERLOOK

Cliff Spring

CLIFF SPRING

ANGELS WINDOW

Zoroaster Temple

CAPE ROYAL

0   1 mi

0   1 km

Freya Castle

Scenic Drive

© MOON.COM

South Rim

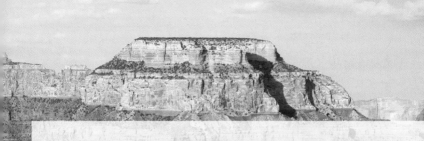

SOUTH RIM

The most popular section of the park by far, the South Rim *is* the Grand Canyon for most visitors. To the west of the magical Grand Canyon Village, the center of all life and activity on the rim with its lodges, shops, restaurants, and lookouts, the park stretches west along the Hermit Road to a series of developed lookouts, each offering a different perspective on the canyon. To the east of the village, the Desert View area presents a wider view of the canyon and the meandering river, reached by driving the paved two-lane Desert View Drive through the evergreen forest, moving farther into natural solitude with every mile.

But as you stare at the canyon from places like Hopi Point, Powell Point, Hermit's Rest, and atop the sublime Desert View Watchtower, high above the inner gorge where the Colorado River continues its sculpting ways, you may find yourself challenged by the Grand Canyon's size. You simply must come here, breathe in the clean, high-country air, feel the warm wind rising out of the gorge, and witness the mystery for yourself.

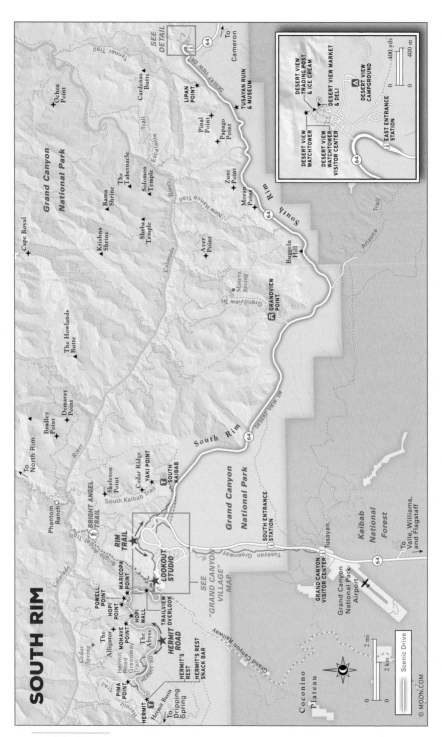

SOUTH RIM

Grand Canyon National Park

SEE DETAIL

To Cameron

Tanner Trail

Ochoa Point

Cardenas Butte

LIPAN POINT

TUSAYAN RUIN & MUSEUM

DESERT VIEW DR

Pinal Point

Papago Point

Escalante Trail

Krishna Shrine

Rama Shrine

The Tabernacle

Solomon Temple

Sheba Temple

Zuni Point

Moran Point

South Rim

64

Cape Royal

Colorado River

New Hance Trail

Ayer Point

Buggeln Hill

Arizona Trail

The Howlands Butte

Miners Spring

GRANDVIEW POINT

Grandview Trail

To North Rim

Bradley Point

Demaray Point

South Rim

64

DESERT VIEW DR

Phantom Ranch

BRIGHT ANGEL TRAIL

Skeleton Point

Cedar Ridge

YAKI POINT

SOUTH KAIBAB

South Kaibab Trail

Grand Canyon National Park

SOUTH ENTRANCE STATION

Kaibab National Forest

To Valle, Williams, and Flagstaff

Colorado River

Bright Angel Trail

RIM TRAIL

LOOKOUT STUDIO

MARICOPA POINT

POWELL POINT

HOPI POINT

HOPI WALL

The Abyss

TRAILVIEW OVERLOOK

HERMIT'S ROAD

SEE "GRAND CANYON VILLAGE" MAP

Tusayan Greenway

Tusayan

GRAND CANYON VISITOR CENTER

Grand Canyon National Park Airport

Cedar Spring

The Alligator

MOHAVE POINT

Hermit Road Greenway Trail

PIMA POINT

Hermit Trail

HERMIT RD

HERMIT ROAD

HERMIT'S REST

HERMIT'S REST SNACK BAR

HERMIT

Hermit Basin

To Dripping Spring

Grand Canyon Railway

Coconino Plateau

Scenic Drive

2 mi

2 km

0

64

DETAIL

400 yds

400 m

0

DESERT VIEW TRADING POST & ICE CREAM

DESERT VIEW MARKET & DELI

DESERT VIEW CAMPGROUND

DESERT VIEW WATCHTOWER

DESERT VIEW WATCHTOWER VISITOR CENTER

EAST ENTRANCE STATION

© MOON.COM

TOP 3

⭐ **1. LOOKOUT STUDIO:** Admire historic national park architecture, shop for the perfect souvenir, watch a California condor soar, and take in some of the best views in the park (page 47).

⭐ **2. HERMIT ROAD:** Hike, ride a bike, or take a shuttle bus on this 14-mile (22.5-km) round-trip excursion to seven different viewpoints, ending at the enchanting Hermit's Rest (page 49).

⭐ **3. RIM TRAIL:** Mostly paved and relatively flat, the Rim Trail passes all the South Rim's must-sees, including a dozen named viewpoints and innumerable hidden perches (page 56).

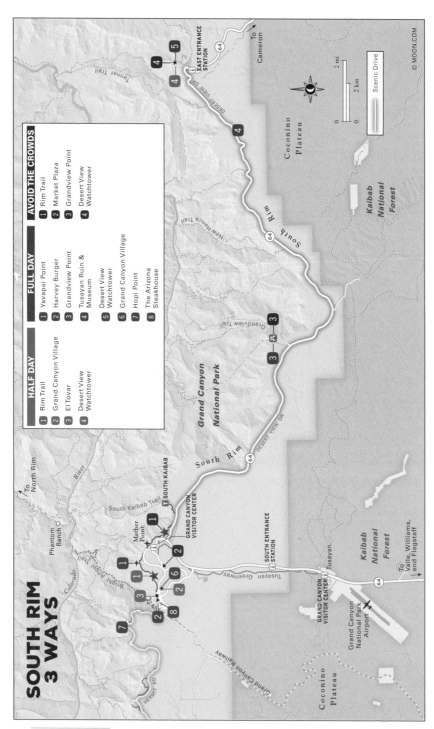

SOUTH RIM
3 WAYS

HALF DAY

1 Rim Trail
2 Grand Canyon Village
3 El Tovar
4 Desert View Watchtower

FULL DAY

1 Yavapai Point
2 Harvey Burger
3 Grandview Point
4 Tusayan Ruin & Museum
5 Desert View Watchtower
6 Grand Canyon Village
7 Hopi Point
8 The Arizona Steakhouse

AVOID THE CROWDS

1 Rim Trail
2 Market Plaza
3 Grandview Point
4 Desert View Watchtower

© MOON.COM

2 mi

2 km

Scenic Drive

SOUTH RIM 3 WAYS

HALF DAY

1   Arrive by 9am so you can park in the main parking lots near the visitor center. Walk the **Rim Trail** between Mather Point (located near the visitor center) and Grand Canyon Village (2 mi/3.2 km), stopping at the visitor center, the Yavapai Geology Museum, and the Trail of Time along the way.

2   Explore **Grand Canyon Village,** looking for California condors from the porch of Lookout Studio, and learning about the history of the park and the region while gazing at the great gorge from various points.

3   Have lunch at historic **El Tovar Dining Room,** located in Grand Canyon Village, then walk or take a shuttle back to the visitor center.

4   Exit the park at the East Entrance so you can drive through the Desert View area and stop at the amazing **Desert View Watchtower** on your way out.

FULL DAY

If you have a full day and it's your first time on the South Rim, follow the Best Day in Grand Canyon itinerary on page 10. If you're making a return trip and/or you have a second day on the South Rim, here are some suggestions:

1 Get up early to watch the sunrise over the canyon at **Yavapai Point** along the Rim Trail. (Tip: If you are not an early riser, plan to watch the sunset at the end of the day.)

2 Have breakfast at **Harvey Burger** at the Bright Angel Lodge.

3 Hop in your car and head east along Desert View Drive to **Grandview Point** (13.4 mi/21.6 km, 25 minutes). Spend time gazing at the canyon from this site, which is where the first tourist hotel on the rim once stood and close to where the Hopi first introduced Spanish explorers to the great gorge. For the best views hike a short distance down the Grandview Trail, whose trailhead is at the point.

4 Continue east on Desert View Drive to the **Tusayan Ruin & Museum** (10.6 mi/17 km, 18 minutes). Peruse the collection of artifacts and take a self-guided walking tour of the ruin (0.1 mi/0.2 km), encountering the ancient cultures of the Grand Canyon's Indigenous peoples and the awesome landscape that inspired them.

5 Get back on Desert View Drive for 3.4 miles (5.5 km, about 7 minutes) to the **Desert View Watchtower.** Walk through and explore the tower, climbing the stairs and viewing the amazing Hopi art on the walls. Make sure to go out on the veranda for an overpowering view of the canyon. If you're hungry, grab lunch at the nearby Desert View Market and Deli.

6 Drive back to **Grand Canyon Village** (24.5 mi/39.4 km) on Desert View Drive, stopping to view the canyon from Lipan Point and Moran Point along the way. Back in Grand Canyon Village, rest up and prepare for an early evening hike along the rim.

7 Time your hike for sunset (pack a headlamp). Start behind the Bright Angel Lodge and head west on the Rim Trail 2.2 miles (3.5 km) one-way to **Hopi Point.** Join the crowd watching the sunset and then hike back to the village.

8 Have a well-earned dinner and sample the Arizona-made beer and wine at **The Arizona Steakhouse** in the village.

AVOID THE CROWDS

Even on the popular South Rim, early risers will often find themselves alone or among just a few of their own kind, and the rim-side world is fresh and magical first thing the in morning. Plan your South Rim trip for winter (Jan.-Mar.) when it's cooler, sometimes snowy, and far less crowded than in summer.

1 Start with a morning hike on the **Rim Trail,** hiking from Mather Point toward the South Kaibab Trailhead (2.4 mi/3.9 km one-way). There are far fewer people on the outer edges of this 13-mile (20.9-km) trail along the rim. When you've reached the South Kaibab trailhead, turn around and hike back to the village (or take a shuttle).

2 It's relatively easy to get away on your own at the viewpoints; it's the eateries where crowding can sometimes be a problem. To avoid this, pack your own food and picnic. At **Market Plaza** you'll find everything you need for an elegant al fresco meal.

3 Drive out to the lesser-visited Desert View section of the park on Desert View Drive (23 mi/37 km one-way), stopping to picnic at **Grandview Point.**

4 After lunch, continue on Desert View Drive past Moran and Lipan points before encountering the star attraction: the glorious **Desert View Watchtower.**

More Ways to Avoid the Crowds

- Bring your bike (or rent one inside the park at Bright Angel Bicycles) and ride the **Hermit Road** and the **Hermit Road Greenway Trail** to **Hermit's Rest** (7.4 mi/11.9 km one-way). To avoid long lines at the entrance station, park outside the boundaries and ride in on the **Tusayan Greenway.**

- Tusayan Ruin & Museum

- Lipan Point

- Desert View Drive

- Hermit Trail to Dripping Spring

HIGHLIGHTS

MATHER POINT

As most South Rim visitors enter through the park's South Entrance, it's no surprise that the most visited viewpoint in the park is the first one along that route—Mather Point, named for the first National Park Service director, Stephen T. Mather. While crowded, Mather Point offers a typically astounding view of the canyon and is probably the mind's-eye view that most casual visitors take away. It can get busy, especially in the summer. Park at one of the four large lots near the visitor center complex and walk the short paved path from the **Grand Canyon Visitor Center.** At Mather Point you can walk out onto two railed-off jutting rocks to feel like you're hovering on the edge of an abyss, but you may have to stand in line to get right up to the edge.

YAVAPAI GEOLOGY MUSEUM

928/638-7890; 8am-8pm daily summer, 8am-6pm daily winter

Yavapai Geology Museum and Observation Station is the best place in the park to learn about the canyon's geology. This Kaibab limestone and ponderosa pine museum and bookstore is a must-visit for visitors interested in learning about what they're seeing.

Designed by architect Herbert Maier and first opened in 1928, the building itself is of interest. Like the buildings of Mary Jane Colter—the architect and designer who helped the Fred Harvey Company create the South Rim's distinctive aesthetic—the stacked-stone structure merges with the rim itself to appear a foregone and inevitable part of the landscape. It's cool in here in the summer and

Mather Point

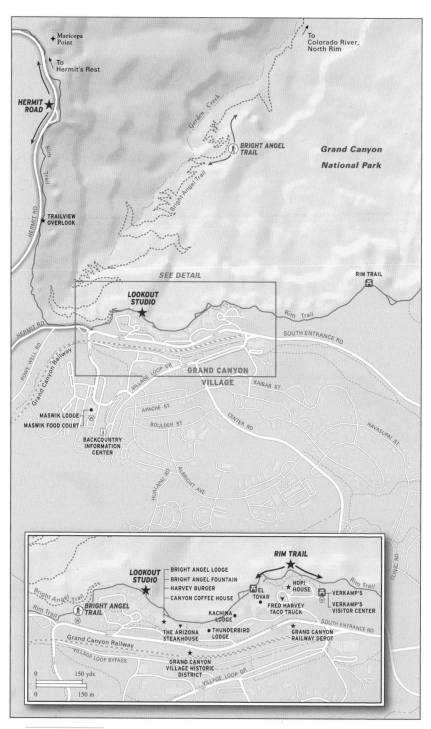

Maricopa
Point

To
Hermit's Rest

To
Colorado River,
North Rim

Garden Creek

HERMIT
ROAD

Rim Trail

HERMIT RD

TRAILVIEW
OVERLOOK

Bright Angel Trail

BRIGHT ANGEL
TRAIL

Grand Canyon

National Park

SEE DETAIL

RIM TRAIL

LOOKOUT
STUDIO

Rim Trail

HERMIT RD

ROWE WELL RD

Grand Canyon Railway

VILLAGE LOOP DR

GRAND CANYON
VILLAGE

SOUTH ENTRANCE RD

KAIBAB ST

MASWIK LODGE
MASWIK FOOD COURT

APACHE ST

BOULDER ST

CENTER RD

HAVASUPAI ST

BACKCOUNTRY
INFORMATION
CENTER

HUALAPAI RD

ALBRIGHT AVE

CLINIC RD

RIM TRAIL

LOOKOUT
STUDIO

BRIGHT ANGEL LODGE
BRIGHT ANGEL FOUNTAIN
HARVEY BURGER
CANYON COFFEE HOUSE

HOPI
HOUSE

EL TOVAR

VERKAMP'S

Rim Trail

Bright Angel Trail

BRIGHT ANGEL
TRAIL

Rim Trail

KACHINA
LODGE

FRED HARVEY
TACO TRUCK

VERKAMP'S
VISITOR CENTER

THE ARIZONA
STEAKHOUSE

THUNDERBIRD
LODGE

SOUTH ENTRANCE RD

Grand Canyon Railway

GRAND CANYON
RAILWAY DEPOT

VILLAGE LOOP BYPASS

GRAND CANYON
VILLAGE HISTORIC
DISTRICT

VILLAGE LOOP DR

0   150 yds

0   150 m

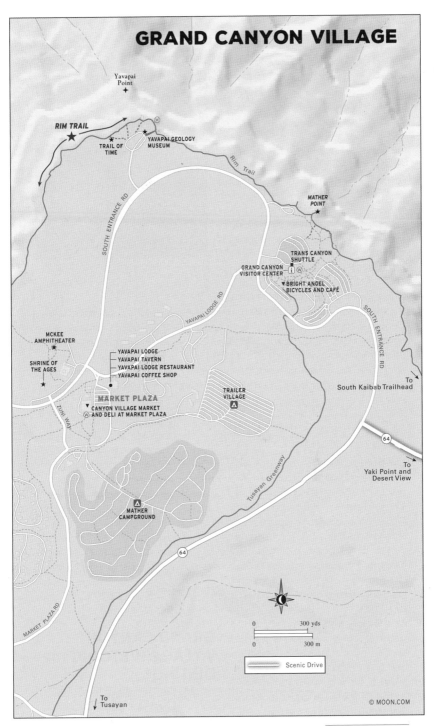

GRAND CANYON VILLAGE

Yavapai
Point

RIM TRAIL

TRAIL OF
TIME

YAVAPAI GEOLOGY
MUSEUM

Rim Trail

MATHER
POINT

SOUTH ENTRANCE RD

TRANS CANYON
SHUTTLE

GRAND CANYON
VISITOR CENTER

BRIGHT ANGEL
BICYCLES AND CAFÉ

YAVAPAI LODGE RD

SOUTH ENTRANCE RD

MCKEE
AMPHITHEATER

SHRINE OF
THE AGES

To
South Kaibab Trailhead

YAVAPAI LODGE
YAVAPAI TAVERN
YAVAPAI LODGE RESTAURANT
YAVAPAI COFFEE SHOP

TRAILER
VILLAGE

MARKET PLAZA

ZUNI WAY

CANYON VILLAGE MARKET
AND DELI AT MARKET PLAZA

64

To
Yaki Point and
Desert View

Tusayan Greenway

MATHER
CAMPGROUND

64

MARKET PLAZA RD

0   300 yds

0   300 m

Scenic Drive

To
Tusayan

© MOON.COM

TRAIL OF TIME

After you've opened and flipped through Grand Canyon's wide-open geologic storybook at Yavapai Point, pick up the wheelchair-accessible Trail of Time just outside the little stacked-rock museum building. A 2.8-mile (4.6-km) geologic timeline on the Rim Trail, the Trail of Time is a great way to put all that information into perspective while strolling along the rim. Each meter of the trail has a distinctive marker that equals one million years, and along the way there are rocks, viewing tubes, and exhibits explaining the incredible formation of Grand Canyon. If you walk from Yavapai to the village

Trail of Time marker

(1.3 mi/2.1 km, about 1 hour; the pamphlet *A Journey Through Time: Grand Canyon Geology* is available at both ends), you move backward in time toward the oldest rocks in Grand Canyon. The rocks of the Elves Chasm gneiss, part of the Vishnu basement rocks of the inner gorge, are about 1,840 million years old. Heading east from the village to Yavapai takes you forward in time toward the canyon's youngest rocks, Kaibab limestone, just 270 million years old.

warm in the winter. It's a place where time is easily lost, where you enter the gorge's timelessness, and you may even forget that you are in a museum while staring through the large windows that face the canyon. That's because you're not really in a museum, but rather an observation station. The site for the station, **Yavapai Point,** was handpicked by top geologists as the best for viewing the various strata and receiving a rim-side lesson on the region's geologic history and present. It's also a great place to see the sunset and sunrise over the canyon, with long and open views of both the east and west, a large parking lot nearby, and a central location near Grand Canyon Village.

The museum features myriad displays about canyon geology. Particularly helpful is the huge topographic relief map of the canyon—a giant's-eye view that really helps you discern what you're seeing once you turn into an ant outside on the rim.

You can reach the museum by walking 0.8 mile (1.3 km) west from the visitor center or taking the shuttle bus on the Orange Route. There's also a small parking lot and bathrooms.

GRAND CANYON VILLAGE HISTORIC DISTRICT

Largely the creation of the Santa Fe Railroad and National Park Service architects in the early 1900s, Grand Canyon Village today is a diverse and enchanting assemblage of historic buildings still in use. The stylishly rustic village, which includes out-of-sight residential neighborhoods for park and concessionaire employees, has some 247 structures and is listed as a National Historic Landmark District. It's the center of the South Rim, and the busy area between El Tovar and Bright Angel Lodge is something of a town square.

Hopi House

A few steps from the front porch of El Tovar is Mary Jane Colter's Hopi House, designed and built in 1905, and meant to look like the traditional structures that still stand on the Hopi Mesas to the east of the Grand Canyon. Hopi workers used local materials to build this unique gift shop and gallery for Native American art. The Fred Harvey Company even hired the famous Hopi-Tewa potter Nampeyo to live here with her family while demonstrating her artistic talents and Hopi lifeways to tourists. This is one of the best places in the region for viewing and buying Hopi, Navajo, and Pueblo art (though most of the art is quite expensive), and there are even items made by Nampeyo's descendants on view and for sale here.

Verkamp's

Along the rim just east of El Tovar, Verkamp's was for a century a curio shop run by the Verkamp family, whose founding ancestor started out here selling Native American art and souvenirs to tourists out of a canvas tent. The business, the longest-running family concern in the national park system, closed down in 2008 due mostly to the reluctance of another generation to take it on. Verkamp's is now a Grand Canyon Conservancy bookstore and gift shop with a small museum about the history and growth of Grand Canyon Village. The building, a 1905 modified Mission-style house that is like nothing else on the rim, housed the Verkamp family upstairs until the 1970s and is now on the National Historic Register.

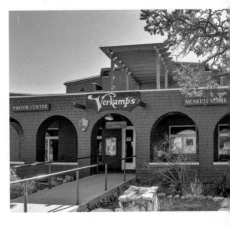

Hopi House (top); Verkamp's (bottom)

SCOUTING FOR CALIFORNIA CONDORS

It seems a bit strange, but one of the best places in canyon country to see a famous California condor soaring above the gorge is in the bustling Grand Canyon Village area in back of **Bright Angel Lodge** and **El Tovar**. Scientists think that the condors gather here, in one of the busiest areas in the entire region, because they are scavengers and used to following great herds in search of food. Whatever the reason, it's thrilling to watch these huge, ancient birds flying over the canyon. One of the best spots in the village to observe them is from the porch of **Lookout Studio,** especially early in the morning and toward evening.

Grand Canyon Railway
800/843-8724; www.thetrain.com

Grand Canyon changed forever when the Santa Fe Railroad came to the South Rim in 1901. Instead of being visited primarily by wealthy tourists willing to pay too much for a punishing stagecoach ride from Flagstaff only to stay in questionable accommodations on the rim, now wealthy and middle-class travelers could travel to the rim with relative ease. The tracks and the trains soon inspired a better class of cabin along the rim, and in 1905 the Santa Fe Railroad built the luxurious El Tovar Hotel. A few years later the railroad decided it needed a new depot to match the hotel's considerable rustic style. Designed by railroad architect Francis W. Wilson, the log structure just down the hill from El Tovar opened in 1909. Today the **Grand Canyon Railway Depot** is the oldest standing wooden train depot in the national park system, a National

Lookout Studio

THE FRED HARVEY COMPANY

It wasn't until the **Santa Fe Railroad** reached the South Rim of the Grand Canyon in 1901 that the great chasm's now-famous tourist trade really got going. Prior to that, travelers faced an all-day stagecoach ride from Flagstaff at a cost of $20, a high price to pay for sore bones and cramped quarters. Thanks to the railroad, even travelers of a less seasoned variety could see the wonders of the West, including the Grand Canyon, with relative ease.

The railroad's main concessionaire, the **Fred Harvey Company,** in those years operated "Harvey House" hotels, restaurants, and lunch counters all along the Santa Fe line. Widely celebrated for their high-quality fare and service, these eateries often became the nicest places in towns that were still little more than frontier outposts. Each Harvey Company restaurant was staffed by the famous **"Harvey Girls,"** young women often recruited in cities, intensively trained as waitresses, and then sent out to work at far-flung spots along the railway. There are today several women who worked as Harvey Girls buried in Grand Canyon's Pioneer Cemetery.

Along with bringing its special brand of service to the South Rim, the Harvey Company in the 1920s and 1930s enlisted the considerable talents of Arts and Crafts designer and architect **Mary Jane Colter** to build lodges, lookouts, galleries, and stores on the South Rim. These treasured buildings still stand today, and are now considered to be some of the finest architectural accomplishments in the entire national park system. The Harvey Company's dedication to simple elegance, and Colter's interest in and understanding of Pueblo Indian architecture and lifeways, created an artful human stamp on the rim that nearly lives up to the breathtaking canyon it serves.

For half a century or more, the Santa Fe line from Williams took millions of tourists to the edge of the canyon. But finally the American love affair with the automobile, the rising mythology of the go-west road trip, and the interstate highway system killed train travel to Grand Canyon National Park by the late 1960s. In the 1990s, however, entrepreneurs revived the railroad as an excursion and tourist line. Today, the **Grand Canyon Railway** carries more than 250,000 passengers to the South Rim every year, which has significantly reduced polluting automobile traffic in the cramped park.

Historic Landmark, and still in service as a train station, hosting hundreds of historic Grand Canyon Railway passengers every day.

★ Lookout Studio

Mary Jane Colter also designed the Lookout Studio, west of the Bright Angel Lodge, a little stacked-stone watch house that seems to be a mysterious extension of the rim itself. The stone patio juts out over the canyon and is a popular place for picture taking. The Lookout was built in 1914 exactly for that purpose—to provide a comfortable but "indigenous" building and deck from which visitors could gaze at and photograph the canyon. It was fitted with high-powered telescopes and soon

Hopi Point

BEST PLACE TO WATCH THE SUNSET

There's some debate about the best viewpoint on the South Rim for gazing at the famous Grand Canyon sunset, but it's an academic argument only; the sun going down over the canyon is a must-see performance from anywhere along the rim. That being said, ask a ranger or a photographer for their recommendation and you will hear **Hopi Point** more often than not. This viewpoint along the Hermit Road juts out from the rim, allowing for sweeping and unobstructed views. What's more, it's a fun place to be around sunset. The site is crowded with visitors from around the globe, but it's a supremely peaceful crowd, awed to whispers by the beauty of the fading sun playing upon the red rocks.

became one of the most popular snapshot scenes on the rim. It still is today, and on many days you'll be standing elbow to elbow with camera-carrying tourists clicking away. As she did with her other buildings on the rim, Colter designed the Lookout to be a kind of amalgam of Native American ruins and backcountry pioneer utilitarianism. Her formula of using found and indigenous materials, stacked haphazardly, works wonderfully here. When it was first built, the little stone hovel was so "authentic" that it even had weeds growing out of the roof. Inside, where you'll find books and canyon souvenirs, the studio looks much as it did when it first opened. The jutting stone patio is still one of the best places from which to view the canyon.

★ HERMIT ROAD

March-November, the park's free shuttle goes all the way to architect and Southwestern-design queen Mary Jane Colter's **Hermit's Rest,** about 7 miles (11.3 km) from Grand Canyon Village along the park's western scenic drive called the Hermit Road. It takes approximately two hours to complete the loop, stopping at nine viewpoints along

the way, including **Trailview Overlook** (1.5 mi/2.4 km from village), **Maricopa Point** (2.7 mi/4.3 km from village), **Powell Point** (3.3 mi/5.3 km from village), **Hopi Point** (2.9 mi/4.7 km from village), **Mohave Point** (4.2 mi/6.8 km from village), **Pima Point** (7.5 mi/12.1 km from village), and, finally, **Hermit's Rest,** a charming stone hovel built to look old and haphazard. Inside there's a gift shop and a snack bar. There are also bathrooms here and access to the Hermit Trail. On the return route, buses stop only at Mohave and Hopi Points.

The Hermit Road viewpoints are some of the best in the park for viewing the sunsets. To make it in time for these dramatic solar performances, catch the bus at least an hour before sunset. There is often a long wait at the **Hermit's Rest Transfer Stop,** just west of the Bright Angel Lodge. The bus drivers generally know the times of sunrise and sunset. The route is open to cars December-February, when you can drive to most of the viewpoints and stare at your leisure.

HOPI POINT

With an expansive and unbounded view, probably the best from the rim (certainly the best from the Hermit Road), Hopi Point gets very busy at sunrise and sunset, so much so that if you don't like crowds it should be avoided during these most popular viewing times. From here catch amazing views of the river and, to the north, the famous mesas named after Egyptian gods: **Isis Temple, Horus Temple,** and **Osiris Temple.** Named for the Hindu god, **Shiva Temple,** an imposing plateau with a forested peak some 7,646 feet high, sits 6 miles (9.6 km) north of Hopi Point looking toward the North Rim. The plateau displays the Grand Canyon's strata well: it's topped with Kaibab limestone over creamy Coconino sandstone, and has slopes and terraces made of the Supai Group, Redwall limestone, and the Tonto group.

There's a small monument here to Colonel Claude Hale Birdseye, who headed the U.S. Geological Survey through the canyon in 1923, which marked the beginning of the drive to dam the Colorado and use its flow and power for profit. This has long been a favorite spot for photographers, and you are likely to see them set up with their tripods. There are restrooms here, too. Don't miss seeing the decommissioned fire lookout along the Hermit Road between Hopi Point and Powell Point.

HERMIT'S REST

The final stop on the Hermit Road is the enchanting gift shop and resthouse called Hermit's Rest, a rest stop designed by Mary Jane Colter in 1914. As you walk up a path past a stacked-boulder entranceway, from which hangs an old mission bell from New Mexico, the little stone cabin comes into view. It is meant to look as if some lonely hermit dug a hole in the side of a hill and then stacked rock on top of rock until something haphazard but cozy rose from the rim—a structure from the realm of fairy tales. Inside, the huge, yawning fireplace, tall and deep enough to be a room itself, dominates the warm, rustic front room, where there are a few chairs chopped out of stumps, a Navajo blanket or two splashing color against the gray stone, and elegant lantern lamps hanging from the rafters. Outside, the views of the canyon and down the Hermit Trail are spectacular, but something about that little rock shelter makes it hard to leave. The large, often quite chubby Grand Canyon ravens seem to be big fans of Colter's rustic and romantic style; this is one of the best places on the South Rim to watch them glide and socialize.

YAKI POINT

The farthest east that the free shuttle will take you, Yaki Point is a fantastic viewpoint and provides access to the South Kaibab Trailhead, which is right next to the viewpoint. The point is about 2 miles (3.2 km) east toward Desert View on AZ 64 near **Pipe Creek Vista.** It's also the eastern terminus or trailhead for the Rim Trail. Yaki Point is at the end of a 1.5-mile (2.4-km) side road that's closed to private vehicles. You can walk there on the Rim Trail or take the free shuttle. If you want to make Yaki Point part of Desert View Drive, you can park your car at a small picnic area just east of the side road, where there are bathrooms and parking, and then cross the road and follow an approximately 0.5-mile (0.8-km) path through the woods to the promontory and the South Kaibab Trailhead. From here you can see Zoroaster Temple, Wotans Throne, and the breathtakingly steep and

Grandview Point (left); Tusayan Ruin & Museum (right)

twisty South Kaibab Trail along Cedar Ridge. The National Park Service built the trail in 1925 to compete with the Bright Angel Trail, on which entrepreneurial prospector-turned-politician Ralph Cameron had a $1 per person stranglehold. A favorite trail of many canyon hikers, the South Kaibab is relatively short but very steep, and it's the quickest corridor route into the inner gorge.

GRANDVIEW POINT

Back in the old pioneer days before the park, Grandview Point, a forested viewpoint along the Desert View Drive, was one of the main tourist areas along the South Rim, home to the Grandview Hotel, opened in 1897. Before that it was the main access point to Ralph Cameron and Pete Berry's Last Chance Mine, far below on Horseshoe Mesa. The two pioneers built what eventually became the **Grandview Trail** leading to the mesa in 1893. Today the trail remains open, but it is a wild and unkempt route into the gorge that is generally used only by experienced canyon hikers. There's a large interpretive sign here that tells the story of the mine and the hotel. While nothing remains of the old hotel, adventurous hikers will find remnants of the mining operation down on Horseshoe Mesa.

TUSAYAN RUIN & MUSEUM

928/638-7888; 9am-5pm daily

The Tusayan Ruin & Museum has a small but interesting group of exhibits on the canyon's early human settlers. The museum is located next to an 800-year-old Ancestral Puebloan ruin with a self-guided trail and regularly scheduled free ranger walks. Since the free shuttle bus doesn't come this far east, you have to drive to the museum and ruin; it's about 3 miles (4.8 km) west of Desert View and 22 miles (35.4 km) east of the village. It's worth the drive, though, especially if you're heading to the Desert View section anyway. The museum has displays on the history of human life in the region along with excellent artifacts of the Hopi, Navajo, Havasupai, and Paiute. Don't miss Roy Anderson's fascinating 1986 painting depicting a romantic vision of life at Tusayan some 800 years ago.

While the canyonlands haven't been exactly hospitable to humans

Lipan Point

over the eons, the oldest artifacts found in Grand Canyon date back about 12,000 years. They include little stick-built animal fetishes found in caves inside the canyon and throughout the Southwest. The ancient Kayenta people constructed and occupied a small village here around AD 1185. The unreconstructed ruin consists of several "rooms" surrounded by low and mostly fallen rock walls, scattered along a 0.1-mile (0.2-km) flat, paved, wheelchair-accessible trail through the pinyon pine forest. The ruin was first excavated in 1930 by Harold S. Gladwin. Archaeologists believe the village included apartments around a large plaza facing south toward the sacred San Francisco Peaks, which was used as a general living area for about 16-20 people, along with several small storage rooms and a kiva—an underground structure used for religious ceremonies. Tusayan is thought to have been the westernmost outpost of the ancient Kayenta people and is linked to other nearby sites such as Keet Seel and White House Ruin on the Navajo Reservation to the east. Follow the short entrance road off Desert View Drive to the native-stone building and parking lot; you'll find bathrooms close by.

Desert View Watchtower

LIPAN POINT

From Lipan Point, a beautiful viewpoint near the Desert View Watchtower, you'll see the rocks from the Grand Canyon Supergroup, tilted formations at the canyon bottom that are some 740-1,200 million years old. From here you'll also see Hance Rapid 3.8 miles (6.1 km) below, the first major rapid below Lees Ferry. The expansive views from here include great looks at the North Rim, the Vermilion Cliffs, and the fertile Unkar Delta far below, where Ancestral Puebloan farmers lived for hundreds of years. Lipan Point is a popular vantage from which to view sunrise and sunset over Grand Canyon.

DESERT VIEW WATCHTOWER

What is perhaps the most mysterious and thrilling of Mary Jane Colter's canyon creations, the Desert View Watchtower (built in 1932) is an artful homage to smaller Ancestral Puebloan-built towers found at Hovenweep National Monument and elsewhere in the Four Corners region, the exact purpose of which is still unknown.

You reach the tower's high, windy deck by climbing the twisting, steep steps winding around the open middle, past walls painted with visions of Hopi lore and religion by Hopi artist Fred Kabotie. From the deck of the watchtower, the South Rim's highest viewpoint, the whole arid expanse opens up, and you feel something like a lucky survivor at the very edge of existence, even among the crowds. Such is the evocative power, the rough-edged romanticism, of Colter's vision.

SCENIC DRIVES

DESERT VIEW DRIVE

DRIVING DISTANCE: 25 miles (40.2 km) one-way
DRIVING TIME: 45 minutes–1 hour without stops
START: Junction of the South Entrance Road and Desert View Drive, Mile Marker 241.5
END: Desert View Drive Mile Marker 264.5

The Desert View driving tour explores the eastern portion of the South Rim; its main draw, other than expansive views of the canyon, is Mary Jane Colter's Desert View Watchtower, the center of the area's action and appeal, about 25 miles (40.2 km) east of Grand Canyon Village. Without stopping at the many developed viewpoints, the drive to the watchtower, campground, and small eateries takes about 45 minutes to an hour; when you add in the many viewpoint stops, the drive could take several hours to most of the day. The viewpoints along this drive, which one ranger called the "quiet side of the South Rim," gradually change from forest to high-country desert, and are typically less crowded than those that can be reached by the shuttle.

The free shuttle goes only as far as **Yaki Point,** a great place to watch the sunrise and sunset, near the popular South Kaibab Trailhead. Yaki Point is at the end of a 1.5-mile (2.4-km) side road northeast of AZ 64. The area is closed to private vehicles, but all the other stops to the east can be reached only by private vehicle. If you want to make Yaki Point part of the Desert View driving tour, you can park your car at a small picnic area just east of the side road (about 2 mi/3.2 km from the village) and then cross the road and follow a path

Yaki Point

for about 0.5 mile (0.8 km) through the woods to the promontory and the South Kaibab Trailhead.

Along Desert View Drive, make sure not to miss the essential **Grandview Point,** where the original canyon lodge once stood long ago. From here the rough Grandview Trail leads below the rim. The viewpoint sits at 7,400 feet (2,256 m), about 12 miles (19.3 km) east of the village and then a mile (1.6 km) on a side road. It's considered one of the grandest views of them all, hence the name; the canyon spreads out willingly from here, and the sunrise in the east hits it strong and happy. To the east, look for the 7,844-foot (2,391-m) monument called the Sinking Ship, and to the north below look for Horseshoe Mesa.

Moran Point, east of Grandview, is just 8 miles (12.9 km) south of Cape Royal (as the condor flies) on the North Rim and offers some impressive views of the canyon and the river (18 mi/28.9 km from village). The point is named for the great painter of the canyon, Thomas Moran, whose brave attempts to capture the gorge on canvas helped create the buzz that led to the canyon's federal protection. Directly below the left side of the point you'll see Hance Rapid, one of the largest on the Colorado. It's 3 miles (4.8 km) away, but if you're quiet you might be able to hear the rushing and roaring.

Farther on Desert View Drive you'll come to **Tusayan Ruin & Museum** (22 mi/35.4 km from village). Stop here for a self-guided walking tour of the small Ancestral Puebloan ruin and a look around the small museum

the Colorado River from Desert View

with exhibits about the rim's ancient inhabitants and the descendants who still call the region home.

As the drive winds down and the trees turn from pine to pinyon to scrub, **Lipan Point** (23.3 mi/37.5 km from village) offers wide-open vistas and the best view of the river from the South Rim. It's a popular Desert View spot for watching the sunrise and sunset, and at times it can get somewhat crowded.

Finally, at Desert View, there's a large parking lot, bathrooms, gift shops, a deli, a gas station, and a campground. From the patio of the amazing, can't-miss **Desert View Watchtower** (25 mi/40.2 km from village), you'll be able to catch a faraway glimpse of sacred Navajo Mountain near the Utah-Arizona border, the most distant point visible from within the park.

Turn around and head back to the village on the same road, stopping again at the viewpoints or just cruising along through the forest.

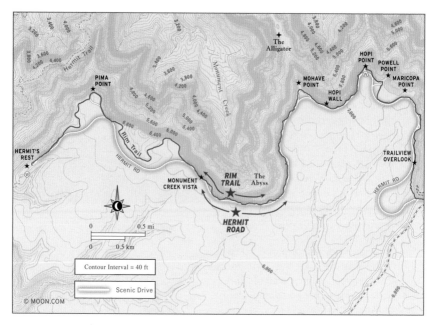

BEST HIKES

★ RIM TRAIL

DISTANCE: 12.8 miles (20.6 km) one-way
DURATION: All day
ELEVATION GAIN: About 200 feet (61 m)
EFFORT: Easy
TRAIL CONDITIONS: Paved except for unpaved stretch between Powell Point and Monument Creek Vista (narrow, packed-dirt path); some steep parts heading west from Bright Angel Lodge to Hermit's Rest
TRAILHEAD: Multiple access points, from South Kaibab Trailhead in the east to Hermit's Rest in the west

If you can manage a nearly 13-mile (20.9-km), relatively easy walk at an altitude of around 7,000 feet (2,134 m), the Rim Trail provides the single best way to see all of the South Rim. The trail, paved for most of its length, runs from the South Kaibab Trailhead area on the east, through the village, and all the way west to Hermit's Rest, hitting every major point of interest and beauty along the way. The path gets a little tough as it rises a bit past the Bright Angel Trailhead just west of the village. Heading farther west, the trail becomes a thin, dirt single-track between Powell Point and Monument Creek Vista, but it never gets too difficult. (You can avoid these sections by walking on the road, which is paved.) It would be considered an easy, scenic walk by just about anybody, kids included. But perhaps the best thing about the Rim Trail is that you don't have to hike the whole 12.8 miles (20.6 km)—far from it. There are at least 16 shuttle stops along the way, and you can hop on and off the trail at your pleasure. Dogs are allowed on the Rim

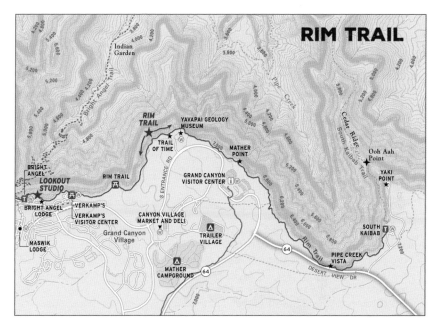

RIM TRAIL

Trail with a leash, but you can't take them on the shuttle buses.

Few will want to hike the entire way, of course. Such an epic walk would in fact require twice the miles (or at least one long ride on the shuttle bus), as the trail is not a loop but a ribbon stretched out flat along the rim from west to east. It's better to pick out a relatively short stretch and take your time.

BRIGHT ANGEL LODGE TO POWELL POINT

DISTANCE: 1.9 miles (3.1 km) one-way
DURATION: 1-2 hours
EFFORT: Easy
TRAIL CONDITIONS: Paved and wheelchair accessible, with a few steeper sections
TRAILHEAD: Bright Angel Lodge
SHUTTLE STOP: Bright Angel Lodge, on Village Route (Blue) / Hermit's Rest Route (Red)

Heading west from Bright Angel Lodge and the village center, the Rim Trail climbs to a long plateau and then hugs the rim all the way to Hermit's Rest, about 7 miles (11.3 km) on. The long, wide, and unobstructed views at Hopi Point make it one of the most popular points from which to view sunset and sunrise.

About 0.5 mile (0.8 km) west from Bright Angel Lodge, you'll rise up to the **Trailview Overlook** and watch hikers descending and ascending the Bright Angel Trail. After traversing the plateau's east side, the trail winds around to face the north across the canyon at **Maricopa Point** (about 0.7 mi/1.1 km west from Trailview Overlook). Just a short walk on and you pass **Powell Point** (0.5 mi/0.8 km west from Maricopa Point), a stunning, unhemmed viewpoint and the site of the Powell Memorial, a monument dedicated to the first modern explorer of the Colorado River through Grand Canyon. The rim in these western regions is dominated by a pygmy forest of pinyon, juniper, and oak, and past Powell Point begin

TOP HIKE
BRIGHT ANGEL TRAIL

DISTANCE: 3-9.6 miles (4.8-15.4 km) round-trip
DURATION: 2-8 hours
ELEVATION GAIN: 3,040 feet (927 m) from trailhead to Indian Garden
EFFORT: Moderate to strenuous
TRAIL CONDITIONS: Narrow, rocky, steep, sandy
TRAILHEAD: Just west of Bright Angel Lodge
SHUTTLE STOP: Bright Angel Lodge, on Village Route (Blue)

Hiking down the Bright Angel Trail, you quickly leave behind the piney rim and enter a sharp and arid landscape, twisting down and around switchbacks on a path that is sometimes all rock underfoot. Step aside for the many mule trains that use this route, and watch for the droppings, which are everywhere. It doesn't take long for the rim to look very far away, and you soon feel like you are deep within a chasm and those rim-top people are mere ants scurrying about.

The Bright Angel Trail is the most popular trail in the canyon owing in part to its starting just to the west of the **Bright Angel Lodge** in the village center. It's considered by park staff to be the safest trail because it has two resthouses with water. The Bright Angel was once the only easily accessible corridor trail from the South Rim, and for years Grand Canyon pioneer Ralph Cameron charged $1 per person to use it. Many South Rim visitors choose to walk down the (now free) Bright Angel Trail a bit just to get a feeling of what it's like to be below the rim. If you want to do something a little more structured, the 3-mile (4.8-km) round-trip hike to the **1.5-Mile Resthouse** is a good introduction to the steep, twisting trail. The going gets tougher on the way to **Three-Mile Resthouse,** a 6-mile (9.7-km) round-trip hike. Both resthouses have water available from mid-May to mid-October, but don't rely on it; breaks in the trans-canyon waterline sometimes shuts them down. One of the best day hikes from the South Rim is the 9.6-mile (15.4-km) round-trip to beautiful **Indian Garden,** a cool and green oasis in the arid inner canyon. This is a rather punishing day hike, not recommended in the summer.

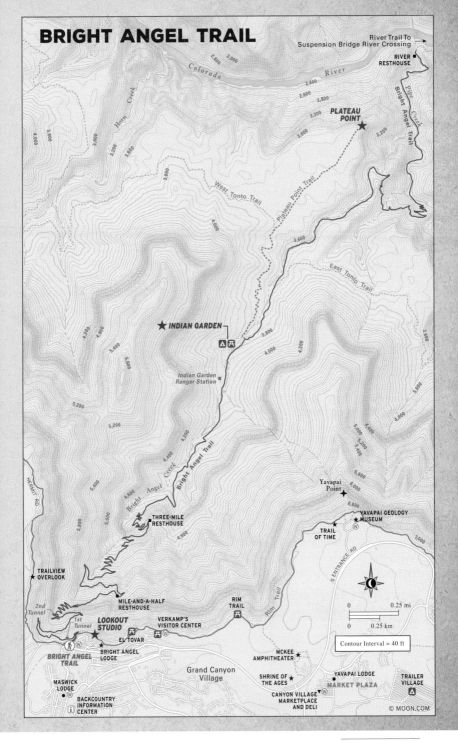

BRIGHT ANGEL TRAIL

River Trail To
Suspension Bridge River Crossing

RIVER
RESTHOUSE

Colorado   River

3,000
2,800

2,400
2,600
2,800
3,200

PLATEAU
POINT
3,200

Horn   Creek

4,000
3,800
3,600
3,200
3,600

3,800

West Tonto Trail

Plateau Point Trail

3,600

Pipe   Creek

Bright Angel Trail

East Tonto Trail

4,000

3,600

INDIAN GARDEN

3,800

4,000

4,200
4,400

Indian Garden
Ranger Station

4,200
4,600

4,800
5,600

5,400

5,200

5,200

4,400
4,200

Bright   Angel   Creek

Bright Angel Trail

4,600

5,400

5,000

Yavapai
Point

4,400
5,000
5,000
5,200

5,600
6,200

Yavapai Point

6,800

7,000

3,800

4,000

HERMIT RD.

5,800

5,000

THREE-MILE
RESTHOUSE

4,800

YAVAPAI GEOLOGY
MUSEUM

TRAIL
OF TIME

TRAILVIEW
OVERLOOK

2nd
Tunnel

1st Tunnel

MILE-AND-A-HALF
RESTHOUSE

LOOKOUT
STUDIO

EL TOVAR

BRIGHT ANGEL
TRAIL

MASWICK
LODGE

BACKCOUNTRY
INFORMATION
CENTER

BRIGHT ANGEL
LODGE

VERKAMP'S
VISITOR CENTER

RIM
TRAIL

Rim   Trail

S ENTRANCE RD.

0   0.25 mi

0   0.25 km

Contour Interval = 40 ft

MCKEE
AMPHITHEATER

Grand Canyon
Village

SHRINE OF
THE AGES

CANYON VILLAGE
MARKETPLACE
AND DELI

YAVAPAI LODGE

MARKET PLAZA

TRAILER
VILLAGE

© MOON.COM

some of the best views of the Colorado snaking far below.

POWELL POINT TO MONUMENT CREEK VISTA

DISTANCE: 3 miles (4.8 km) one-way
DURATION: 1.5-2.5 hours
EFFORT: Easy
TRAIL CONDITIONS: Narrow packed-dirt path, sometimes rocky
TRAILHEAD: Hopi Point
SHUTTLE STOP: Hopi Point, on Hermit's Rest Route (Red)

From Powell Point to Monument Creek Vista, the Rim Trail is a narrow (3-ft/0.9-m-wide) dirt path. It gets a bit more difficult than the paved stretches because of the narrowness and the lack of pavement; it's not accessible to wheelchairs in this section.

It's just a 0.3-mile (0.5-km) walk along the Rim Trail from Powell Point to **Hopi Point,** which offers sweeping views of the western canyon. Moving west from Hopi Point, the trail turns slightly southward while still hugging the rim along the sheer drop called the **Hopi Wall,** and then leads out to a promontory called **Mohave Point,** just above the long red mesa called the **Alligator.** The trail then jogs south again, passing **The Abyss,** a 3,000-foot (914-m) drop straight down.

There are bathrooms at Hopi Point—the last ones before Hermit's Rest at the end of the trail.

MONUMENT CREEK VISTA TO HERMIT'S REST

DISTANCE: 2.8 miles (4.5 km) one-way
DURATION: 1.5-2.5 hours
EFFORT: Easy
TRAIL CONDITIONS: Wide paved road, open to bikes
TRAILHEAD: Monument Creek Vista
SHUTTLE STOP: Monument Creek Vista, on Hermit's Rest Route (Red)

The Rim Trail widens out beginning at Monument Creek Vista and allows bikes for the next 2.8 miles (4.5 km); this section of the trail is called the Hermit Road Greenway. Below, Monument Creek descends to its marriage with the Colorado River. The Rim Trail reaches a promontory called **Pima Point** (1.8 mi/2.9 km from Monument Creek Vista) and then turns south following the rim, showing Hermit Creek and the Hermit Trail in the side canyon. At **Hermit's Rest** (1 mi/1.6 km from Pima Point), the enchanting gift shop and snack bar designed in the 1930s by Mary Jane Colter, you can catch the free shuttle bus back to the village (it will take at least 30 minutes to an hour to reach the village, as the shuttle buses stop at all the viewpoints on the way there and back). Or you can rest a bit here and then walk back to the village on the Rim Trail.

BRIGHT ANGEL LODGE TO MATHER POINT

DISTANCE: 2.5 miles (4 km) one-way
DURATION: 1.5-2.5 hours
EFFORT: Easy
TRAIL CONDITIONS: Paved and wheelchair accessible
TRAILHEAD: Bright Angel Lodge
SHUTTLE STOP: Bright Angel Lodge, on Village Route (Blue)

Heading east on the Rim Trail from Bright Angel Lodge takes in all the essential sights within **Grand Canyon Village,** follows the **Trail of Time,** and then makes an important stop at **Yavapai Geology Museum and Observation Station** (1.8 mi/2.9 km from the lodge), the must-see

Pima Point (left); Yavapai Observation Station (right)

geology museum and viewpoint that puts the amazing views you're seeing into some kind of approachable perspective. Continuing east along the forested stretch of the Rim Trail leads to **Mather Point** (0.7 mi/1.1 km east of Yavapai), the busiest viewpoint on the South Rim, from which it's a short and easy side stroll to the Grand Canyon Visitor Center and the shuttle bus station.

MATHER POINT TO SOUTH KAIBAB TRAILHEAD
DISTANCE: 2.4 miles (3.9 km) one-way
DURATION: 1.5-2 hours
EFFORT: Easy
TRAIL CONDITIONS: Paved and wheelchair accessible
TRAILHEAD: Mather Point, near Grand Canyon Visitor Center
SHUTTLE STOP: Mather Point, on Rim Route (Orange)

The 2.4-mile (3.9-km) stretch of Rim Trail from Mather Point to the South Kaibab Trailhead passes along a wild section of rim with few developed viewpoints or stops. It's just you, the canyon, and the condors, which can often be seen gliding and diving around **Pipe Creek Vista,** about

1.5 miles (2.4 km) from Mather Point. The Rim Trail ends (and begins) at the parking lot for Yaki Point and the South Kaibab Trailhead. Here the South Kaibab Trail begins its precipitous drop to the river, and you can take a short walk out to Yaki Point for another inspiring view. There are bathrooms here as well as a shuttle bus stop.

SOUTH KAIBAB TRAIL
DISTANCE: 1.8-6 miles (2.9-9.7 km) round-trip
DURATION: 1-6 hours
ELEVATION GAIN: 2,040 feet (622 m) from trailhead to Skeleton Point
EFFORT: Moderate to strenuous
TRAIL CONDITIONS: Narrow, rocky, very steep, sandy in places; mule traffic, mule leavings
TRAILHEAD: Near Yaki Point on the East Rim
SHUTTLE STOP: Yaki Point, on Rim Route (Orange)

Steep but relatively short, the 7-mile (11.3-km) South Kaibab Trail provides the quickest, most direct route from the South Rim to and from the river. It's popular with day hikers and those looking for the quickest way into the gorge, and many consider it

South Kaibab Trail (left); Hermit Trail (right)

superior to the often-crowded Bright Angel Trail. The trailhead is located a few miles east of the village near Yaki Point, which is closed to private vehicles; take the shuttle bus on the Kaibab/Rim Route (Orange).

The 1.8-mile (2.9-km) round-trip hike to **Ooh Aah Point** has great views of the canyon from steep switchbacks. A common turnaround point for day hikers, **Cedar Ridge** is a 3-mile (4.8-km) round-trip hike. If you are interested in a longer haul, the 6-mile (9.7-km) round-trip hike to **Skeleton Point,** from which you can see the Colorado River, is probably as far along this trail as you'll want to go in one day, though in summer you might want to reconsider descending that far.

There's no water anywhere along the trail, and there's no shade to speak of. Bighorn sheep have been known to haunt this trail, and you might feel akin to those dexterous beasts while hiking the rocky ridgeline, which seems unbearably steep in a few places, especially on the way back up. Deer and California condors are also regular residents of the South Kaibab Trail. This is a trail the mules use, so make sure to step aside and wait while the mule trains pass.

HERMIT TRAIL TO DRIPPING SPRING

DISTANCE: 6.2 miles (10 km) round-trip
DURATION: 5-7 hours
ELEVATION GAIN: 1,600 feet (488 m)
EFFORT: Strenuous
TRAIL CONDITIONS: Rock and dirt, sand in some places, narrow, steep, technical
SHUTTLE STOP: Hermit's Rest

Built by the Santa Fe Railroad as a challenge to the fee-charging keeper of the Bright Angel Trail, the Hermit Trail just past Hermit's Rest leads to some less visited areas of the canyon. This trail isn't maintained with the same energy as the well-traveled corridor trails, and it has no potable water.

The trailhead for the Hermit Trail is just west of Hermit's Rest, which is 7 miles (11.3 km) west of Grand Canyon Village via the Hermit Road. For most of the year Hermit Road is closed to private vehicles, so a day hike in this section of the park typically requires a 30-minute to one-hour one-way shuttle bus trip to

Hermit's Rest and then a short walk to the trailhead. A permit for a backpacking trip down the Hermit Trail allows you to drive to the trailhead and leave your vehicle, no matter the season.

The 6.2-mile (10-km) round-trip hike to the secluded and green **Dripping Spring** is one of the best day hikes in the canyon for midlevel to expert hikers. Start out on the Hermit Trail's steep, rocky, almost stair-like switchbacks. You come to the Waldron Trail Junction after 1.3 miles (2.1 km). Look for the **Dripping Spring Trailhead** after about 0.2 mile (0.3 km) from the Waldron Trail Junction, once you reach a more level section dominated by pinyon pine and juniper. Veer left (west) on the trail, which begins to rise a bit and leads along a ridgeline across **Hermit Basin;** the views are so awe-inspiring that it's difficult to keep your eyes on the skinny trail. After about 1 mile (1.6 km), you'll come to the junction with the Boucher Trail. Continue heading west, hiking about 0.5 mile (0.8 km) up a side canyon to the cool and shady rock overhang known as Dripping Spring. And it really does drip: A shock of fernlike greenery creeps off the rock overhang, trickling cold spring water at a steady pace into a small collecting pool (don't drink without treating it). Get your head wet, have a picnic, and kick back in this out-of-the-way, hard-won oasis. But don't stay too long. The hike back up is nothing to take lightly: The switchbacks are punishing, and the end, as it always does when one is hiking up a trail in the Grand Canyon, seems to get farther away as your legs begin to gain fatigue-weight. There's no water on the trail, so make sure to bring enough along and conserve it.

BACKPACKING

On any given night there are only a few hundred visitors sleeping below the rim—at Phantom Ranch, a Mary Jane Colter-designed lodge near the mouth of Bright Angel Canyon; at three developed campgrounds along the corridor trails; or off somewhere in the canyon's wild primitive labyrinth. Until a few decades ago backpacking into the inner canyon was something of a free-for-all, but these days access to the interior is strictly controlled through a permit system.

PERMITS

To camp overnight below the rim, you have to purchase a **permit** ($10, plus $8 pp per night), and they're not always easy to get—each year the park receives about 30,000 requests for backcountry permits and issues only about 13,000. The earlier you apply for a permit the better; the earliest you can apply is 10 days before the first of the month four months before your proposed trip date. The easiest way to get a permit is to go to the **park's website** (www.nps.gov/grca), print out a backcountry permit request form, fill it out, and then fax it first thing in the morning on the date in question—for example, if you want to hike in October, you would **fax** (928/638-2125) your request May 20-June 1. Have patience; on the first day of the month the fax number is usually busy throughout the day—keep trying. On the permit request form you'll indicate at which campgrounds you will stay. The permit is your reservation. For more information on obtaining a backcountry permit, call the **South Rim Backcountry Information Center** (928/638-7875; 8am-noon and 1pm-5pm daily).

CORRIDOR TRAILS

Rangers divide Grand Canyon's rim-to-river and inner-canyon backpacking trails into **four zones—Corridor, Threshold, Primitive,** and **Wild**—based on several factors. The **corridor trails**—Bright Angel, South Kaibab, and North Kaibab (which starts on the North Rim)—are well maintained and signed, easy to follow, and patrolled, and backpackers have seasonal access to potable water, toilets, ranger stations, and emergency phones.

A **classic South Rim corridor trail backpacking trip** (4 days, 3 nights, 19.5 mi/31 km) starts on the **South Kaibab Trail,** on which you descend quickly to the inner gorge and stop for two nights at Bright Angel Campground, a shady creek-side spot between the Colorado River and Phantom Ranch. On the third day, break camp early and hike up the **Bright Angel Trail** to Indian Garden. Camp here and hike 3 miles (4.8 km) round-trip to Plateau Point for an inspiring view of the gorge and the river. Set out early the next morning for the final leg up the Bright Angel Trail to the South Rim.

BIKING

There are about 13 miles (20.9 km) of roads and greenways through the park that allow bikes, including a route from the Grand Canyon Visitor Center to Grand Canyon Village, and routes from the village to Mather Campground and Market Plaza—basically anywhere you need to go inside the park.

Hermit Road
7 miles (11.3 km) one-way

While the main park roads are open to bikes, they don't have wide shoulders or bike lanes. The exception is Hermit Road, which is closed to cars March-November. Seven miles (11.3 km) one-way between the village and the western end of the park

Tusayan Greenway (left); Hermit Road Greenway Trail (right)

TUSAYAN GREENWAY

Drive past the Grand Canyon Visitor Center in Tusayan, south of Grand Canyon National Park, and take a left from the traffic circle up the road to the **Tusayan Greenway** trailhead. Park your rig, unload the bikes, and start riding. You are now on your way to the very rim of Grand Canyon, riding a smooth and worthy human-powered machine over the undulating forest terrain where others have struggled astride mule, horse, tour bus, or motorhome. You are the future of the national parks while they are long past.

Yes, it's a 6.5-mile (10.5-km) one-way ride, trending uphill but not to an outlandish degree. Look out for wildlife as you race through the forest on the paved trail with the pine-scented breeze tickling your smiling face. However, you can also leave your car at the visitor center in Tusayan and, with your bike in tow, catch the **free shuttle bus** a few steps away (Tusayan Route or Purple Route). Or if you decide to ride into the park, you can always leave on a shuttle bus with your bike, or vice versa.

Pick up a *South Rim Pocket Map & Services Guide* when you enter the park (or download and print one in advance) and note all the green dotted routes. These are the park's bike trails, aka greenways. Stick to these and the park roads and you'll easily get wherever you want to go. Don't forget to bring a bike lock.

For a **fun biking day trip** at the South Rim (about 32 mi/51.5 km of riding round-trip), leave your car at the Tusayan Greenway trailhead outside the park; ride the greenways into and across the park, making stops at the main visitor center, Market Plaza, and Grand Canyon Village along the way; and then ride the 7-mile (11.3-km) Hermit Road all the way to Hermit's Rest, including the 2.8-mile (4.5-km) Greenway Trail along the rim. To get back to your car, head out of the park the same way you came in.

at Hermit's Rest, the Hermit Road is the best and most popular bikeway on the South Rim. The only traffic you'll have to deal with on this rolling ride of tough ups and fun downs is the occasional shuttle bus. Just pull over and let them pass.

Hermit Road Greenway Trail
2.8 miles (4.5 km) one-way
Bikes are not allowed on the Rim Trail except for a 2.8-mile (4.5-km) section called the Hermit Road Greenway Trail. The paved trail begins at Monument Creek Vista along the Hermit Road and ends close to Hermit's Rest.

This is about as close as you can get to the rim on a bike, and it's a fun and beautiful stretch of trail highly recommended to bicyclists. To get to the very edge of the rim, you have to park your bike and walk a bit, but never very far, and there are bike racks at each developed viewpoint.

Rentals
BRIGHT ANGEL BICYCLES AND CAFÉ
10 S. Entrance Road; 928/814-8704; **www.bikegrandcanyon.com; 6am-8pm daily Apr.-Nov., 7am-7pm daily Dec.-Mar.**
Bright Angel Bicycles and Café rents

comfortable, easy-to-ride bikes as well as safety equipment and trailers for the tots. It also offers bike tours of varying length and difficulty. Bright Angel Bicycles is located next to the Grand Canyon Visitor Center, near the South Entrance.

FOOD

Most of the in-park eateries are certified green restaurants (certified by the Green Restaurant Association) and strive to serve dishes using local and organic produce and meats. Foodies, food-lovers, and world-class diners should not miss a stop at El Tovar.

STANDOUTS
El Tovar Dining Room
928/638-2631, ext. 6432; www. grandcanyonlodges.com; 6:30am-11am, 11:30am-2pm, and 5pm-10pm daily; reservations highly recommended

El Tovar Dining Room truly carries on the Fred Harvey Company traditions on which it was founded in 1905. A serious, competent staff serves fresh, creative, locally inspired and sourced dishes in a cozy, mural-lined dining room that has not been significantly altered from the way it looked back when Teddy Roosevelt and Zane Grey ate here. The wine, entrées, and desserts are all top-notch and would be appreciated anywhere in the world—but they always seem to be that much tastier with the sun going down over the canyon. Pay attention to the specials, which usually feature some in-season local edibles; they are always the best thing to eat within several hundred miles in any direction.

Harvey Burger
928/638-2631; www.grandcanyon-lodges.com; 6:30am-10pm daily

Harvey Burger, just off the Bright Angel Lodge's lobby, is a perfect place for a big, hearty breakfast before a day hike below the rim. It

El Tovar

serves all the standard, rib-sticking dishes amid decorations and ephemera recalling the Fred Harvey heyday. At lunch there's stew, chili, salads, sandwiches, and burgers, and for dinner there's steak, pasta, and fish dishes called "Bright Angel Traditions," along with a few offerings from The Arizona Steakhouse's menu.

BEST PICNIC SPOTS
Rim Trail

There aren't many picnic tables along this 13-mile (20.9-km) east-west trail along the rim, but there are benches, and any one of them makes a good place for a picnic if you don't mind balancing your sandwich on your knees.

Grandview Point
East of the Visitor Center along the Desert View Road

Grandview Point, where it's said that Hopi guides first showed the great canyon to the Spanish conquistadores, has a few picnic tables, bathrooms, and a grand view to go with your outdoor feast.

Verkamp's Visitor Center and El Tovar

There are a few picnic tables just east of Verkamp's Visitor Center, and benches suitable for picnicking on the covered porch of El Tovar. Either spot offers good spots to enjoy a hot dog or burrito purchased from the Fred Harvey Food Truck, which parks most days between El Tovar and Hopi House in Grand Canyon Village.

Amphitheater near Mather Point
west of Moran Point

A short stroll from Moran Point, the small amphitheater along the rim has rustic bench seating and is often uncrowded even in this typically crowded area.

Desert View Market and Deli (top); Yavapai Lodge (middle); a picnic bench in Grand Canyon Village (bottom)

SOUTH RIM FOOD OPTIONS

NAME	LOCATION/SHUTTLE STOP	TYPE
Bright Angel Bicycles and Café	Near main visitor center	take-out
Fred Harvey Food Truck	Near El Tovar	take-out
★ El Tovar Dining Room	Grand Canyon Village	sit-down restaurant
The Arizona Steakhouse	Grand Canyon Village	sit-down restaurant
★ Harvey Burger	Grand Canyon Village	sit-down restaurant
Bright Angel Fountain	Grand Canyon Village	take-out
The Canyon Coffee House	Grand Canyon Village	take-out
Maswik Food Court	Grand Canyon Village	cafeteria-style
Hermit's Rest Snack Bar	Hermit's Rest	take-out
Yavapai Lodge Restaurant	Market Plaza	cafeteria-style
Yavapai Tavern	Market Plaza	sit-down restaurant
Yavapai Coffee Shop	Market Plaza	take-out
Canyon Village Market and Deli	Market Plaza	take-out
Desert View Market and Deli	Desert View	take-out
Desert View Trading Post & Ice Cream	Desert View	take-out

FOOD	PRICE	HOURS
deli food	budget	6am–8pm daily Apr.–Nov., 7am–7pm daily Dec.–Mar.
Mexican	budget	11am–4pm daily (weather dependent)
contemporary American	moderate	6:30am–11am, 11:30am–2pm, 5pm–10pm daily; reservations recommended
Southwestern	moderate	11:30am–3pm and 4:30pm–10pm daily Mar.–Oct., 4:30pm–10pm daily Nov.–Dec.
classic American	moderate	6:30am–10pm daily
ice cream and snacks	budget	11am–5pm daily in season
coffee and snacks	budget	6am–10am daily
classic American	budget	6am–10pm daily
sandwiches and snacks	budget	8am–8pm daily spring–fall, 9am–5pm daily in winter
American and Southwestern	moderate	6am–10pm daily
pub food	budget	noon–10pm daily
coffee and snacks	budget	6am–3pm daily
sandwiches and groceries	budget	8am–8pm daily
sandwiches and groceries	budget	8am–8pm daily Mar. 23–Sept. 3, 8am–6pm daily Sept. 4–Oct. 21, 9am–5pm daily Oct. 22–Mar. 22
ice cream and sweets	budget	8am–8pm daily Mar. 23–Sept. 3, 8am–6pm daily Sept. 4–Oct. 21, 9am–5pm daily Oct. 22–Mar. 22

SOUTH RIM CAMPGROUNDS

NAME	LOCATION/SHUTTLE STOP	SEASON
★ Mather	Market Plaza	year-round
Desert View	Desert View	May-mid-Oct.
Trailer Village RV Park	Market Plaza	year-round

CAMPING

There are three in-park campgrounds on the South Rim. Mather Campground and Trailer Village are close to the village and all the action, while the Desert View Campground, about 25 miles (40 km) east of the village, is on the quieter side of the park.

Reservations

Reserve campsites as far ahead of time as possible.

Tips

At 7,000 feet (2,134 m), the forested South Rim can get chilly at night even in the summer, so plan accordingly. Mather Campground has wheelchair-accessible sites, but Trailer Village and Desert View Campground do not.

STANDOUTS
Mather Campground
877/444-6777; www.recreation.gov
Mather Campground takes reservations up to six months ahead for the March-November 20 peak season and thereafter operates on a first-come, first-served basis. Located near the village and offering more than 300 basic campsites with grills and fire pits, the campground typically fills up by about noon during the summer busy season. It has restrooms with showers, and coin-operated laundry machines. The campground is open to tents and trailers but has no hookups and is closed to RVs longer than 30 feet (9.1 m). Even if you aren't an experienced camper, a stay at Mather is a fun and inexpensive alternative to sleeping indoors. Despite its large size and crowds, the campground gets pretty quiet at night. Even in summer, the night takes on a bit of a chill, making a campfire not exactly necessary but not out of the question. Bring your own wood or buy it at the store nearby. A large, clean restroom and shower facility is within walking distance from most

SITES AND AMENITIES	RV LIMIT	PRICE	RESERVATIONS
272 tent and RV sites, 55 tent-only sites; flush toilets; potable water; showers; no hookups	30 ft (9.1 m)	$18 Mar.-Nov., $15 Dec.-Feb.	yes, required Mar.-Nov. (recreation.gov); first-come, first-served Dec.-Feb.
50 tent and RV sites; flush toilets; potable water; no hookups	30 ft (9.1 m)	$18	yes, required (recreation.gov)
123 RV sites; flush toilets; potable water; electric hookups; dump station	50 ft (15.2 m)	$61-71	yes (www.visitgrandcanyon.com)

sites, and they even have blow-dryers. Everything is coin operated, and there's an office on-site that gives change. Consider bringing bikes along, especially for the kids. The village is about a 15-minute walk from the campground on forested, paved trails, or you can take the free shuttle from a stop nearby. Pets are allowed but must be kept on a leash, and they're not allowed on shuttle buses.

Mather Campground

SOUTH RIM LODGING

NAME	LOCATION/SHUTTLE STOP	SEASON
★ El Tovar	Grand Canyon Village	year-round
★ Bright Angel Lodge	Grand Canyon Village	year-round
Kachina Lodge	Grand Canyon Village	year-round
Thunderbird Lodge	Grand Canyon Village	year-round
Maswik Lodge	Market Plaza	year-round
Yavapai Lodge	Market Plaza	year-round

LODGING

There are six lodges within Grand Canyon National Park at the South Rim—five operated by **Xanterra** (www.grandcanyonlodges.com) and one, Yavapai Lodge, operated by **Delaware North** (www.visitgrand-canyon.com). The hotels within the park are a green and sustainable choice: Xanterra and Delaware North both have robust sustainability programs aimed at conserving water and energy, reducing pollution, and increasing recycling while decreasing use of landfills.

All the hotels within Grand Canyon National Park offer wheelchair-accessible rooms.

STANDOUTS
El Tovar
303/297-2757 or 888/297-2757;
www.grandcanyonlodges.com
A stay at El Tovar, one of the most distinctive and memorable hotels in the state, would be the secondary highlight—after the gorge itself—of any trip to the South Rim. Opened in 1905, the log-and-stone National

Historic Landmark, standing about 20 feet (6.1 m) from the rim, has 78 rooms and suites. The hotel's restaurant serves some of the best food in Arizona for breakfast, lunch, and dinner, and there's a comfortable cocktail lounge off the lobby with a window on the canyon. A mezzanine sitting area overlooks the log-cabin lobby, and a **gift shop** sells Native American art and crafts as well as canyon souvenirs. If you're looking to splurge on something truly exceptional, there's a honeymoon suite overlooking the canyon.

Bright Angel Lodge
303/297-2757 or 888/297-2757;
www.grandcanyonlodges.com
When first built in the 1930s, the Bright Angel Lodge was meant to serve the middle-class travelers then being lured by the Santa Fe Railroad, and it's still affordable and comfortable while retaining a rustic character that fits perfectly with the wild canyon just outside. Lodge rooms don't have TVs, and most have

OPTIONS	PRICE
hotel rooms and suites	rooms starting at $217; suites starting at $442
hikers rooms with shared showers, lodge rooms, and cabins	rooms starting at $95
hotel rooms	rooms starting at $225
hotel rooms	rooms starting at $225
motel rooms	rooms starting at $215
hotel rooms	rooms starting at $150

only one bed. The utilitarian "hikers" rooms have refrigerators and share several private showers, which have lockable doors and just enough room to dress. Bright Angel is the place to sleep before hiking into the canyon; you just roll out of bed onto the Bright Angel Trail. The lodge's cabins just west of the main building have private baths, TVs, and sitting rooms; these include two cabins created out of historic pioneer structures, Buckey O'Neill's Log Cabin and Red Horse Station. Drinking and dining options include a small bar and coffeehouse, a Harvey House diner, and a restaurant with big windows framing the canyon.

Bright Angel Lodge

INFORMATION AND SERVICES

Grand Canyon Village is the hub of activity in the South Rim, home to lodges, shops, and restaurants. Most of the quotidian services on the South Rim are at **Market Plaza,** where there's a general store, **Chase Bank** and an ATM (foreign currency exchange for bank members only; 928/638-2437), a **post office** (928/638-2512), and **free Wi-Fi** in the **Canyon Village Market and Deli** (8am-8pm daily). There are also **ATMs** in the lobbies of the Bright Angel Lodge, El Tovar, and Maswik Lodge.

Entrance Stations

You can purchase your park pass ahead of time at www.recreation.gov or https://yourpassnow.com, the visitor centers in Flagstaff and Williams, the Chevron Travel Stop in Valle, or at the Grand Canyon Visitor Center in Tusayan, but doing so does not allow you to skip the lines unless you also ride the shuttle bus into the park rather than taking your car.

South Entrance

AZ 64

The vast majority of visitors to Grand Canyon National Park enter through the South Entrance Station on AZ 64 from **Williams,** or via U.S. 180 to AZ 64 from **Flagstaff.** There are several lanes and generally the lines keep moving; however, on summer and holiday weekends you may experience a significant wait. As you enter a ranger will give you a *South Rim Pocket Map & Services Guide,* which is a helpful reference for exploring the park.

Desert View (East) Entrance

AZ 64 enters the park through the south but soon veers east toward Navajoland and the much smaller and considerably less busy **East Entrance Station,** in the park's **Desert View** section, about 25 miles (40.2 km) east of Grand Canyon Village. This route is a good choice for those who want a more leisurely and comprehensive look at the rim, as there are quite a few stops along the way to the village that you might not otherwise get to if you enter through the South Entrance. To reach the East Entrance Station, take U.S. 89 for 46 miles (74 km) north of **Flagstaff,** across a wide, big-sky landscape covered in volcanic rock, pine forests, and yellow wildflowers, to Cameron, on the Navajo Reservation. Then head west on AZ 64 for about 30 miles (48.3 km) to the entrance station. This is the best way to leave the park's South Rim section if you are heading to the Navajo or Hopi Reservations, or to the North Rim and Zion and Bryce Canyon in southern Utah.

Visitor Centers

Grand Canyon Visitor Center

7am-6pm daily May-Sept., 9am-4pm daily Oct.-Apr.

While Historic Grand Canyon Village is the heart of the South Rim, Mather Point and Grand Canyon Visitor Center, about 2.2 miles (3.5 km) east of the village along the rim, provide easy and in-depth introductions to the canyon and the park. Entering from the main South Entrance on AZ 64 from Williams or Flagstaff, keep to the South Entrance Road for 5.1 miles (8.2 km) to reach four large parking lots around the visitor center complex. During the high season and on holidays, these parking lots can fill up by 9:30am, and most days they fill up by 10am regardless of the season. If you can't find parking here, proceed to Market Plaza and then Park Headquarters to find a spot; you can then backtrack to the visitor center via the Rim Trail or the free shuttle bus. Entering from the east through the Desert View area, turn right onto South Entrance Road at its junction with Desert View Drive, about 23 miles (37 km) from the East Entrance. From the junction it's only 1 mile (1.6 km) on the South Entrance Road to the main visitor center.

In the visitor center, you will find a water refill station, bathrooms, a bookstore with souvenirs and supplies, and a large, light-filled building with information about Grand Canyon and environs. Rangers staff the center all day to answer questions and help you plan your visit, and they offer ranger-led walks, hikes, and natural-history presentations around the park most days and evenings. A 20-minute film shown here on the hour and half hour, *Grand Canyon: A Journey of Wonder*, narrated by the great Peter Coyote, depicts the canyon's dawn-to-dusk cycle of mystery and beauty, and there are several maps and other exhibitions that explain and illuminate the somewhat confusing grandeur just outside.

Verkamp's Visitor Center

8am-7pm daily early Mar.-mid-May and early Sept.-Nov., 8am-8pm daily mid-May-mid-Aug., 9am-8pm daily mid-Aug.-early Sept., 8am-6pm daily Dec.-early Mar.

In Grand Canyon Village, along the rim about 2.2 miles (3.5 km) west of Grand Canyon Visitor Center, is the smaller Verkamp's Visitor Center, near Hopi House and El Tovar. It began in a white-canvas tent when Grand Canyon National Park opened and was a famous curio and souvenir shop right on the rim for 100 years. Since 2015 the historic building has housed a visitor center run by the Grand Canyon Conservancy, which includes books, souvenirs, and displays about the history of Grand Canyon Village.

Desert View Watchtower Visitor Center

9am-5pm daily

The farthest-flung of all the park's South Rim information and visitor centers is in the Desert View Watchtower, about 25 miles (40 km) east of Grand Canyon Village. It is staffed with helpful rangers who have information about Desert View and the rest of the park.

TRANSPORTATION
Getting There

The majority of Grand Canyon visitors drive here, reaching the South Rim from either **Flagstaff** or **Williams** and entering the park through the south or east gates. The South Entrance is usually the busiest, and during the summer traffic is likely to be backed up somewhat.

From the South Entrance

The Grand Canyon Visitor Center, Mather Point, and the main parking lots come into view 4.8 miles (7.7 km) from the South Entrance. After entering the park, simply stay on **AZ 64/South Entrance Road.** Park here if you can find a spot (it's often full after 10am) and use the free shuttles or the Rim Trail to explore the park.

From the East Entrance

To reach the Grand Canyon Visitor Center, Mather Point and the main parking lots from the East Entrance in Desert View, follow **AZ 64** west for 21.7 miles (34.9 km) and then turn right on **South Entrance Road.** From there it's about 0.4 mile (0.6 km) to the lots.

From the North Rim

The epic drive from the North Rim to the South Rim is 210 miles (338 km) long and takes about four hours. From the North Rim section of the park take **AZ 67** 44 miles (70.8 km) to **U.S. 89A** at Jacob Lake. From Jacob Lake drive 56 miles (90.1 km) though the Arizona Strip and cross the Colorado River at Navajo Bridge to pick up **U.S. 89** at Bitter Springs, on the Navajo Nation. From Bitter Springs take **U.S. 89** 57 miles (91.7 km) to Cameron, where you'll pick up **AZ 64** west to the South Rim's East Entrance Station. From there it's 22 miles (35.4 km) to the Grand Canyon Visitor Center via Desert View Drive and South Entrance Road.

From Grand Canyon West

The South Rim is about 239 miles (384.6 km) from Grand Canyon West, on the Hualapai Nation. The drive takes about four hours. From Grand Canyon West take **Diamond Bar Road** and **Stockton Hill Road** 69 miles (111 km) and pick up

Interstate 40 at Kingman. Get on I-40 headed east to Williams, about 113 miles (181.9 km, Exit 165). Take AZ 64 north about 50 miles (80.5 km) to the South Entrance Station.

Bus Tours

Xanterra, the park's main concessionaire, offers in-park **motorcoach tours** (303/297-2757 or 888/297-2757; www.grandcanyonlodges.com; $70 pp adults, $30 pp kids 3-16). Options include sunrise and sunset tours, and longer drives to the eastern Desert View area and the western reaches of the park at Hermit's Rest. This is a comfortable, educational, and entertaining way to see the park, and odds are you will come away with a few new friends—possibly even a new email pal from abroad. Only pay for a tour if you like being around a lot of other people and listening to mildly entertaining banter from the tour guides for hours at a time. It's easy to see and learn about everything the park has to offer without spending extra money on a tour; as in most national parks, the highly informed and friendly rangers hanging around the South Rim's sites offer the same information that you'll get on an expensive tour, but for free. Also, if you like being on your own and getting out away from the crowds, a tour is not for you. To book a tour through Xanterra, you can either plan ahead and book online, or when you arrive check at the activities desk at Maswik and Bright Angel Lodges, from which the tours begin.

Shuttles

The park operates excellent **free shuttle services** along the South Rim, with comfortable buses fueled by compressed natural gas. It's strongly encouraged you park your car for the duration of your visit and use the shuttle. It's nearly impossible to find parking at the various sights, and traffic through the park is not always easy to navigate—there are a lot of one-way routes and oblivious pedestrians that can lead to needless frustration. Make sure

you pick up a free *Pocket Map,* which has a map of the various shuttle routes and stops, available at the entrance gate and at most visitor centers throughout the park.

Pretty much anywhere you want to go in the park a shuttle will get you there, and you rarely have to wait more than 10 minutes at any stop. That being said, there is no shuttle that goes all the way to the Tusayan Ruin & Museum or the Desert View Watchtower near the East Entrance.

Shuttle drivers are a good source of information about the park. They are generally very friendly and knowledgeable, and a few of them are genuinely entertaining. The shuttle conveniently runs from around sunup until about 9pm, and drivers always know the expected sunrise and sundown times and seem to be intent on getting people to the best overlooks to view these two popular daily park events.

Park shuttles have racks that fit 2-3 bikes. All shuttle buses are wheelchair accessible (up to 30 in/76 cm wide and 48 in/122 cm long), with wheelchair ramps and low entrances and exits.

If you are in a hurry to get somewhere, the free shuttle bus is not what you need. Especially during the summer and on spring and early fall weekends, expect to stand in a line and watch several buses fill and depart before you get on.

The year-round **Kaibab/Rim Route (Orange)** will take you from Grand Canyon Visitor Center west to Yavapai Geology Museum and back, and east to the South Kaibab Trailhead, Yaki Point, and Pipe Creek Vista and back. Ride the year-round **Village Route (Blue)** west from the visitor center to Market Plaza, Shrine of the Ages, the Grand Canyon Railway Depot, Bright Angel Lodge, and the Hermit's Rest Route transfer area. Eastbound the Village Route goes from the transfer area to Maswik Lodge, the Backcountry Information Center, Shrine of the Ages, Mather Campground, Trailer Village, Market Plaza, and then back to the visitor center.

The **Hermit's Rest Route (Red)** runs

shuttle on Hermit Road

March–November (Dec.–Feb. Hermit Road is open to private vehicles) and is the way most visitors reach the must-see western viewpoints along the South Rim. The route starts at the Village Route transfer area at the head of Hermit Road and heads west, stopping at Trailview Overlook, Maricopa Point, Powell Point, Mohave Point, The Abyss, Monument Creek Vista, Pima Point, and Hermit's Rest. Headed back east it makes stops only at Pima Point, Mohave Point, and Powell Point before returning to the Village Route transfer.

Parking

The best way to explore Grand Canyon National Park's South Rim is to park your car near a shuttle stop and use a combination of walking and riding the free shuttle to get around. First try the four lots around the **main visitor center,** which include trailer and RV parking spots. In the high season these large parking lots generally fill up by 10am. Next move on to **Market Plaza,** where you can park cars, trailers, and RVs in a large lot, and then the mid-sized lot at **Park Headquarters** across from Market Plaza, where you can park an RV up to 22 feet (6.7 m) long. Both of these lots usually fill up by noon. There are a number of parking spots within the village outside Bright Angel Lodge and El Tovar, but you'll be lucky to get one of these prime spots, which are typically all taken by 2pm. The **Backcountry Information Center** (928/638-7875) also has a large parking lot, the southern portion of which can accommodate RVs and trailers. This lot across the train tracks from the village typically fills by 2pm.

Gas

The closest gas station to Grand Canyon Village is Conoco in Tusayan (928/638-2608), about 7 miles (11.3 km) to the south. There's a gas station in the park's Desert View section, about 26 miles (41.8 km) east of the village.

North Rim

NORTH RIM

Standing at Bright Angel Point on Grand Canyon's North Rim, crowded together with several other gazers as if stranded on a jetty over a wide, hazy sea, someone whispers, "It looks pretty much the same as the other rim."

It's not true—far from it—but the comment brings up the main point about the North Rim: Should you go? Only about 10 percent of canyon visitors make the trip to the North Rim, which is significantly less developed than the South; there aren't many activities other than gazing, unless you are a hiker and a backcountry wilderness lover. The coniferous mountain forests of the Kaibab Plateau are themselves worth the trip—broken by grassy meadows and painted with summer wildflowers, and dappled with aspens that turn yellow and red in the fall and burst out of the otherwise uniform dark green like solitary flames. You may also catch sight of elk and mule deer. But it is a long trip, and you need to be prepared for a land of scant services. In return, you'll find the simple, contemplative pleasures of nature in the raw.

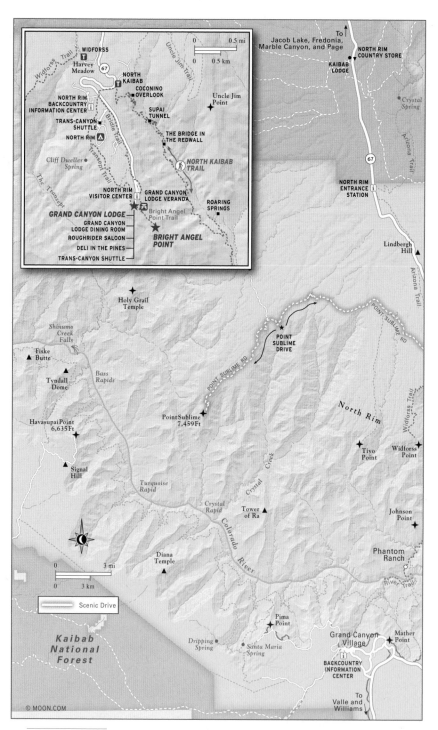

Inset map (North Rim detail):

0   0.5 mi
0   0.5 km

WIDFORSS

Widforss Trail

Harvey Meadow

67

NORTH KAIBAB

COCONINO OVERLOOK

Uncle Jim Trail

Uncle Jim Point

NORTH RIM BACKCOUNTRY INFORMATION CENTER

SUPAI TUNNEL

TRANS-CANYON SHUTTLE

NORTH RIM

Bright Angel Point Trail

THE BRIDGE IN THE REDWALL

Transept Trail

Cliff Dweller Spring

NORTH KAIBAB TRAIL

NORTH RIM VISITOR CENTER

GRAND CANYON LODGE VERANDA

ROARING SPRINGS

GRAND CANYON LODGE

GRAND CANYON LODGE DINING ROOM

ROUGHRIDER SALOON

DELI IN THE PINES

TRANS-CANYON SHUTTLE

The Transept

Bright Angel Point Trail

BRIGHT ANGEL POINT

Main map:

To Jacob Lake, Fredonia, Marble Canyon, and Page

NORTH RIM COUNTRY STORE

KAIBAB LODGE

Crystal Spring

Arizona Trail

67

NORTH RIM ENTRANCE STATION

Lindbergh Hill

Holy Grail Temple

POINT SUBLIME RD

POINT SUBLIME DRIVE

POINT SUBLIME RD

Shinumo Creek Falls

Fiske Butte

Bass Rapids

North Rim

Tyndall Dome

Widforss Trail

Point Sublime 7,459 Ft

Havasupai Point 6,635 Ft

Tivo Point

Widforss Point

Crystal Creek

Signal Hill

Turquoise Rapid

Crystal Rapid

Tower of Ra

Johnson Point

Colorado River

Phantom Ranch

Diana Temple

River Trail

Pima Point

Grand Canyon Village

Mather Point

Dripping Spring

Santa Maria Spring

BACKCOUNTRY INFORMATION CENTER

Kaibab National Forest

3 mi

3 km

Scenic Drive

To Valle and Williams

© MOON.COM

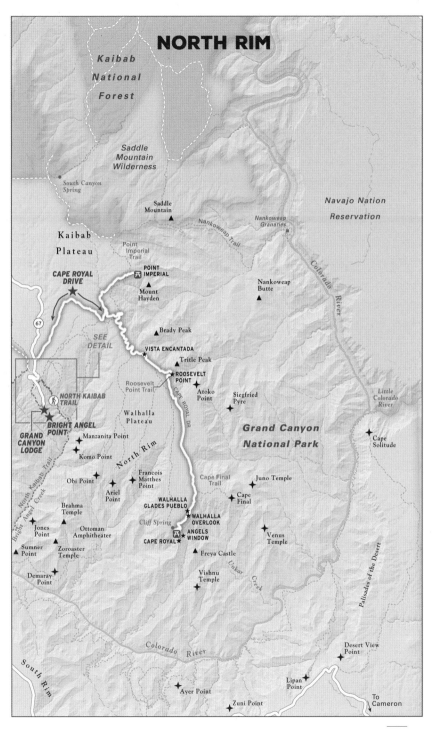

NORTH RIM

Kaibab

National

Forest

*Saddle
Mountain
Wilderness*

South Canyon
Spring

Saddle
Mountain ▲

Nankoweap Trail

Nankoweap
Granaries

Navajo Nation

Reservation

Kaibab

Plateau

Point
Imperial
Trail

**POINT
IMPERIAL**

Nankoweap
Butte ✦

**CAPE ROYAL
DRIVE** ★

Mount
Hayden ▲

67

Brady Peak ✦

*SEE
DETAIL*

VISTA ENCANTADA
★

Tritle Peak ✦

Colorado River

**NORTH KAIBAB
TRAIL** 🚶

**ROOSEVELT
POINT** ★

Roosevelt
Point Trail

Atoko
Point ✦

Siegfried
Pyre ✦

Little
Colorado
River

**BRIGHT ANGEL
POINT** ★

*Walhalla
Plateau*

CAPE ROYAL DR.

*Grand Canyon
National Park*

**GRAND
CANYON
LODGE** ★

✦ Manzanita Point

✦ Komo Point

North Rim

✦ Cape
Solitude

Obi Point ✦

✦ Ariel
Point

Francois
Matthes
Point ✦

Cape Final
Trail

Juno Temple ✦

Brahma
Temple ▲

Ottoman
Amphitheater

Jones
Point ▲

Cliff Spring

**WALHALLA
GLADES PUEBLO**
★

Cape
Final ✦

Sumner ▲
Point

Zoroaster
Temple ▲

**WALHALLA
OVERLOOK** ★

**ANGELS
WINDOW** ★

Venus
Temple ✦

Demaray
Point ✦

CAPE ROYAL 🏕 ★

✦ Freya Castle

Unkar Creek

Vishnu
Temple ✦

Palisades of the Desert

Bright Angel Creek

North Kaibab Trail

Colorado River

South Rim

Desert View
Point ✦

Ayer Point ✦

Lipan
Point ✦

*To
Cameron*

Zuni Point ✦

TOP 3

⭐ **1. BRIGHT ANGEL POINT:** Take a short stroll on a narrow stone peninsula to this premier North Rim gazing spot, and let the Grand Canyon's beauty overwhelm you (page 89).

⭐ **2. CAPE ROYAL DRIVE:** Drive 23 miles (37 km) through the evergreen forest to the far edge of the Walhalla Plateau, stopping at rim-side viewpoints and trails along the way (page 95).

⭐ **3. GRAND CANYON LODGE:** Find a seat on the sunny veranda of this stylishly rustic lodge, and discuss the mind-bending view with fellow adventurers from around the world (page 114).

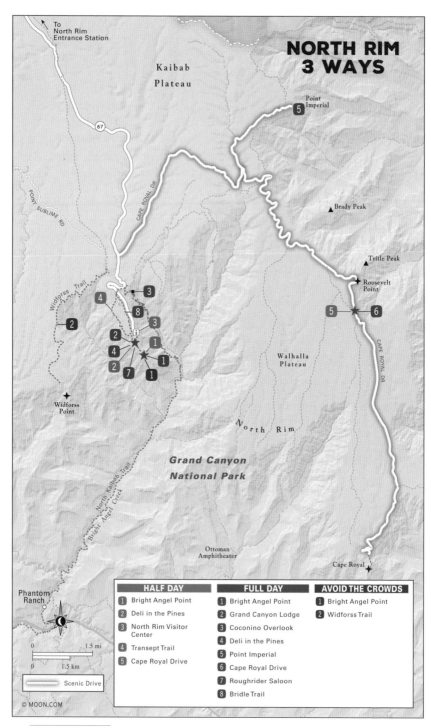

NORTH RIM 3 WAYS

To North Rim Entrance Station

Kaibab Plateau

67

POINT SUBLIME RD

CAPE ROYAL DR

Point Imperial 5

Brady Peak ▲

Tritle Peak ▲

Roosevelt Point ✦

5 ★ 6

CAPE ROYAL DR

Widforss Trail

2

4

3

8

3

2

1

4 ★

2 1

7 ★ 1

Widforss Point ✦

Walhalla Plateau

North Rim

Grand Canyon National Park

North Kaibab Trail

Bright Angel Creek

Ottoman Amphitheater

Cape Royal ✦

Phantom Ranch

HALF DAY	FULL DAY	AVOID THE CROWDS
1 Bright Angel Point	1 Bright Angel Point	1 Bright Angel Point
2 Deli in the Pines	2 Grand Canyon Lodge	2 Widforss Trail
3 North Rim Visitor Center	3 Coconino Overlook	
4 Transept Trail	4 Deli in the Pines	
5 Cape Royal Drive	5 Point Imperial	
	6 Cape Royal Drive	
	7 Roughrider Saloon	
	8 Bridle Trail	

0   1.5 mi
0   1.5 km

▬▬▬ Scenic Drive

© MOON.COM

NORTH RIM 3 WAYS

HALF DAY

1   Take an early morning walk out to **Bright Angel Point** (0.3 mi/0.4 km one-way from the Grand Canyon Lodge) and other viewpoints.

2   Grab a breakfast burrito from the **Deli in the Pines** (located next to Grand Canyon Lodge), then enjoy it on the veranda of the historic lodge.

3   Check out the **North Rim Visitor Center** and the gift shop (located next to the to the lodge).

4   Hike along the **Transept Trail** (3 mi/4.8 km round-trip) between the lodge and the campground, exploring the rim-side forest with the canyon almost always in view.

5   Head out on the **Cape Royal Drive** (23 mi/37 km one-way), stopping at the various viewpoints and trailheads along the way.

FULL DAY

1 Get up early to greet the morning and the vast magical Grand Canyon from the edge of the world at **Bright Angel Point** (0.3 mi/0.4 km one-way from the Grand Canyon Lodge).

2 Head to the veranda of **Grand Canyon Lodge** with a picnic breakfast, or eat in the lodge dining room (reservation required) at a table by a window, looking out on the waking canyon.

3 For a taste of life below the rim, drive to the North Kaibab Trail (1.5 mi/2.5 km north of the lodge on AZ 67) for a 3-mile (4.8-km) round-trip hike to the **Coconino Overlook.**

4 Return to the lodge area and pick up lunch to go at **Deli in the Pines,** but don't eat it yet—save it for your next stop.

5 **Point Imperial** (11 mi/17.7 km from the visitor center), the highest point on the North Rim, is a dramatic spot for a picnic.

6 Spend several hours exploring the **Cape Royal Drive** (23 mi/37 km one-way), stopping at the various viewpoints and trailheads, ending at the must-see Angels Window and Cape Royal viewpoint.

7 Return to the lodge area and have drinks at **Roughrider Saloon,** followed by dinner in the lodge dining room next door.

8 You might want to just stay in the lodge area, kicking back with a beer or reading with the cool breeze on your forehead and the scent of pine in your nose. But if you still have energy, stroll along the **Bridle Trail,** listening to and watching the flitting forest life and waiting for the sinking sun's last show of the day.

AVOID THE CROWDS

The North Rim has far fewer visitors than the South Rim, which isn't to say that it doesn't get crowded: The most accessible viewpoints and the few services here are concentrated in a relatively cramped area around the lodge, where most visitors spend their time. With the North Rim closed throughout the winter, there isn't really an off-season, but the early fall months might be the next best thing.

1 Rising early, even with the sun itself, is the single best way to avoid the crowds on the North Rim. Watching the sunrise from the rim of the Grand Canyon is a joyous experience, and the highland forest is alive with wild activity in the early hours. Grab your camera and your binoculars and head for **Bright Angel Point,** where you might find yourself alone on the edge of a great mystery.

2 You don't have to hike the entire 10-mile (16-km) round-trip **Widforss Trail** to get away from the crowds on the North Rim; about 1.5 miles (2.4 km) from the trailhead (located 2.7 mi/4.3 km north of the lodge) the side-canyon called the Transept comes into view as the trail skirts the rim, and a quiet gazing spot among rocks and trees awaits.

More Ways to Avoid the Crowds

- As one of the more remote areas in North America, this region offers numerous rare chances to go where few dare to tread—but only if you have the right vehicle. You'll need a high-profile SUV with four-wheel drive to visit off-track spots such as **Point Sublime** and **Tuweep,** both hard-won spots where crowds are rarely an issue.

- Cliff Spring Trail

- Widforss Trail

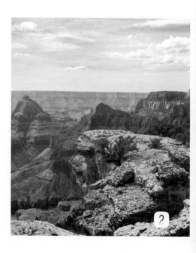

HIGHLIGHTS

★ BRIGHT ANGEL POINT

A kind of natural stone jetty hovering above an empty red-and-green sea, Bright Angel Point (8,161 ft/2,487 m) is the primary North Rim lookout, reached via a paved but somewhat steep 0.3-mile (0.4-km) one-way trail behind Grand Canyon Lodge.

Not only does this often-crowded area provide several jutting views of the canyon (including of Roaring Springs Canyon, the side canyon called the Transept, and on a clear day the South Rim), it also offers the perfect vantage from which to view the lodge as it looms above like a natural extension of the rim itself. About 4.5 miles (7.2 km) to the south, look for **Brahma Temple,** a 7,851 peak that rises above Phantom Ranch in Bright Angel Canyon. This huge rock monument shows off the canyon's strata particularly well. It's capped with Coconino and Kaibab limestone, with sloes and terraces of Hermit, Supai, and Redwall. You will not likely be alone in this area. To spend some quality time here without crowds, get up early and watch the new morning sun hit the red rocks covered with dewy evergreens, welcoming the day on the precipice of a hazy labyrinth whose intricacies defy belief.

POINT IMPERIAL

A view to the southeast toward Navajoland and the Painted Desert, Point Imperial is absolutely worth the scenic 11-mile (17.7-km) drive from the visitor center. At 8,803 feet (2,683 m) it's the highest point on the North Rim, providing glimpses for the sharp-eyed of the mouth of the **Little Colorado River,** the imposing canyon cliffs known as **Palisades**

view from Bright Angel Point

of the Desert, and even **Humphreys Peak,** Arizona's highest at 12,633 feet (3,851 m), some 67 miles (108 km) away in the blue distance. Much closer to the rim, you can see the celebrated **Mount Hayden,** an 8,372-foot (2,552-m) white sandstone peak at the end of a long ridge of red dirt. Named for Arizona pioneer businessman Charles T. Hayden (as are many buildings in Tempe and at Arizona State University, both of which he helped establish), the elegantly eroded peak is a frequent subject for North Rim photographers.

Take AZ 67 north from the visitor center and after 3 miles (4.8 km) turn right onto Cape Royal Road. At mile 5.4 (km 8.7) veer left to Point Imperial. The developed viewpoint has parking, bathrooms, picnic tables, and benches for sitting down when the view buckles your knees.

ROOSEVELT POINT

Roosevelt Point, at mile 11.7 (km 18.8) on Cape Royal Road, is named for Teddy Roosevelt, the former U.S. president who loved Grand Canyon and spent time hunting game on the North Rim. A short loop trail (0.2-mi/0.3-km round-trip) provides the best views; take some time here strolling the trail and relaxing on the well-placed benches. Roosevelt Point has awesome views of the eastern canyon off the Walhalla Plateau, a sliver plateau that sits alongside the Kaibab Plateau on its southeast side. Tritle Peak, topped with white Kaibab limestone, rises 8,300 feet (2,500 m) to the east along a ridge that juts out into the canyon. It was named for F. A. Tritle, a territorial governor in 1881-1885 and early owner of the famous Jerome Copper Mine.

WALHALLA OVERLOOK AND WALHALLA GLADES PUEBLO

Stop at Walhalla Overlook, along Cape Royal Road about 18 miles (29 km) from the turnoff, for a view into the history of human life in Grand Canyon and on the North Rim. From here you can see the red deposits at the confluence of Unkar Creek and the Colorado River known as the Unkar Delta. A relatively large group

Walhalla Overlook (top); Walhalla Glades Pueblo (bottom)

of Ancestral Puebloan farmers lived inside the great canyon and worked the delta from about AD 850-1200. During the latter part of this period the people of the Unkar Delta most likely built the Walhalla Glades Pueblo on the rim just across the road from the overlook, occupying it in summer from about AD 1050-1150. This part of the high country is called the Walhalla Plateau, a "peninsula" surrounded on three sides by the canyon that's slightly lower than the rest of the Kaibab Plateau and therefore subject to warmer air and earlier snowmelts, which is likely why the farmers chose this area to build their small summer farming homes and storage rooms. There's a pamphlet describing a self-guided tour of the six-room ruin at the visitor center. All that remains of this once bustling little outpost is a series of low rock walls that outline what used to be the rooms of the pueblo, but with a little imagination it's possible to speculate about what life would have been like for these hardy North Rim pioneers.

ANGELS WINDOW

Along the trail to the Cape Royal viewpoint, you'll pass the amazing natural arch called Angels Window, a squiggly upside-down triangle of sandstone somehow knocked out of an imposing white-rock outcropping. The window is also a perfect frame for a small section of the Colorado River, and you can walk over the rock out to the very edge of the outcropping (on top of the window), which is protected by a railing, for one of the most thrilling views on the North Rim.

TUWEEP

www.nps.gov/grca/planyourvisit/tuweep.htm

A far-flung unit of Grand Canyon National Park, Tuweep includes a high desert rim-side viewpoint, **Toroweap Overlook** (4,552 ft/1,387 m elevation), and a primitive campground. Few visitors make it out to this dry, scrubby country, but those who do report solitude and adventure. A trip here requires a lot of preplanning and the right weather

Angels Window

Toroweap Overlook

entrance to the Tuweep area (left); road to the Tuweep backcountry campground (right)

(dry). Still, if you have the wherewithal and the time to do it safely, a visit to this backcountry spot will not soon be forgotten.

A former haunt of the Paiute, Tuweep (pronounced tu-VEEP) sits 3,000 precipitous feet (914 m) above the Colorado River on a volcanic landform called the Esplanade, between the piney highlands of the plateau and the canyon's scorched desert bottomlands. Toroweap Overlook is less than a mile (1.6 km) across the gorge from the South Rim, over one of the narrowest and deepest parts of the canyon. Just west of the overlook, look for a 5,102-foot (1,555-m) cinder cone called Vulcan's Throne. From the lookout you'll get almost close-up views of the Colorado River below, and if you're lucky you might see a few rafters going by.

Toroweap is a Paiute term meaning, roughly, "dry and barren valley." The word is used to describe the arid flatlands that stretch west along the rim below the plateau and are significantly lower in elevation than the North and South Rims. Tuweep (meaning "earth" in Paiute) was the name of the old ranching and mining settlement in the area, and now refers to this remote area of Grand Canyon National Park.

To cross this brushy volcanic landscape of juniper and pinyon, devoid of water and succor, lonely and now the domain of desert rats, canyon hoppers, and backcountry explorers, you must have a high-clearance vehicle, or better yet a four-wheel drive. Bring along extra water, food, and warm clothing as well as a tire pump, patches, and maybe even a few extra tires, as the route is known to be particularly hard on them. If you get stuck out here, you really can't be sure of getting any help, and don't expect to have cell coverage; you must be prepared for anything.

The easiest and most reliable route to Tuweep starts at the Grand Canyon Lodge on the North Rim. Take AZ 67 and U.S. 89A to Pipe Springs National Monument on the Arizona Strip (87 mi/140 km, 1 hour 40 minutes). From Pipe Springs, continue east for 6 miles (10 km) to County Road 109, the 61-mile (98-km) rough dirt road to Tuweep, which will take you at least 2-3 hours to negotiate.

SCENIC DRIVES

★ CAPE ROYAL DRIVE

DRIVING DISTANCE: 23 miles (37 km) one-way, plus 3-mile (4.8-km) one-way side trip
DRIVING TIME: 2 hours one-way (plus 30-40-minute side trip)
START: Grand Canyon Lodge
END: Cape Royal

This outrageously scenic drive along the rim to Cape Royal is an essential part of the North Rim experience. The paved two-lane road twists and undulates through the green, white, and fire-blackened highland forest of tall and skinny quaking aspen, thick and shaggy conifers, and black stumps and husks of all sizes. There are several developed viewpoints along the rim-side with parking, picnic tables, interpretive signs, and a few rustic benches on which you can sit back and contemplate the views. Plan to spend at least two hours one-way (it's 23 mi/37 km from Grand Canyon Lodge to Cape Royal), and at least another 30-40 minutes at nearby Point Imperial (a 3-mi/4.8-km one-way side trip; the route branches off from Cape Royal Road at mile 5.4/km 8.7). You reach several of the viewpoints via short and easy trails, so plan on doing some walking. Bring water, food, and warm clothing, and make sure that your vehicle is road-ready (no rigs over 30 ft/9.1 m long); there are no services of any kind on this road, though there are small bathrooms at Point Imperial and Cape Royal. Keep a look out for wildlife along this road, especially wild turkeys.

Get an early start and take AZ 67 north from **Grand Canyon Lodge** for 3 miles (4.8 km) to **Cape Royal Road** and turn right. At mile 5.4 (km 8.7) you need to decide whether to veer left to **Point Imperial,** a southeast-facing

Mount Hayden

BEST PLACE TO WATCH THE SUNSET

If you don't mind driving back to the main lodge area after dark, the best place to view the sunset on the North Rim is from **Cape Royal,** about 23 miles (37 km) one-way from Grand Canyon Lodge, at the very edge of the Walhalla Plateau. Here at the end of the Cape Royal Drive you'll find several viewpoints offering different views of the canyon, to the east, south, and west, allowing for optimal viewing of the sunset in all its spreading glory. Leave the park area about two hours before sunset so you can stop at each of the viewpoints along the Cape Royal Drive, ending with the headlining sunset at Cape Royal.

view of the white-rock peak **Mount Hayden** and across the red-and-green canyon to the Painted Desert on Navajoland, or continue on to the right and catch it on the way back. Either way, Point Imperial is a stop that should not be missed. Each viewpoint provides a different perspective on the canyon, so it's best to stop and spend some time at each one.

At mile 8 (km 12.9) is **Greenland Lake,** a beautiful lush meadow with a natural sink that traps rainwater and snowmelt, making this "lake" a highly variable prospect. There's also an old ranching cabin in this

Greenland Lake

peaceful clearing about 200 yards (183 m) off the road, which you can reach by a short dirt trail.

At mile 10 (km 16.1) is **Vista Encantada** ("enchanting view"), which has a gorgeous view and is a great spot for a picnic. Stop here and contemplate another white-tipped, attention-grabbing peak—**Brady Peak,** just east of the picnic spot. The peak was named for Arizona pioneer Peter Brady (no relation to the Brady Bunch), who came to the territory in the impossibly early days of the 1850s and was a longtime elected official. Here you'll also see the often dry Nankoweap Creek etched beige against the red-and-green canyon landscape, and beyond that, if it's a clear day, you may see all the way to Navajoland and the Painted Desert.

Just up the road a bit at mile 11.7 (km 18.8) is **Roosevelt Point,** named for Teddy Roosevelt, the former U.S. president who loved Grand Canyon and spent time hunting game on the North Rim. A short loop trail (0.2 mi/0.3 km round-trip) provides the best views; take some time here strolling the trail and relaxing on the well-placed benches. Roosevelt Point, like Point Imperial and Vista Encantada, has awesome views of the eastern canyon off the **Walhalla**

sunset view from the overlook on Cape Royal

Walhalla Plateau (top); Freya Castle (middle); Unkar Delta region from along the Cape Royal Drive (bottom)

Plateau, a sliver plateau that sits alongside the Kaibab Plateau on its southeast side. **Tritle Peak,** topped with white Kaibab limestone same as Brady and Hayden, rises 8,300 feet (2,530 m) to the east along a ridge that juts out into the canyon. It was named for F. A. Tritle, a territorial governor in 1881–1885 and early owner of the famous Jerome Copper Mine.

At mile 17.2 (km 27.7) you'll come to the **Cape Final Trailhead;** the trail is 4.2 miles (6.8 km) round-trip to a spectacular viewpoint with awesome looks at **Unkar Creek,** the **Painted Desert,** and **Freya Castle,** a sharp peak of Coconino sandstone 7,288 feet (2,221 m) high, named for the Norse goddess. It's situated between Vishnu Temple (7,533 ft/2,296 m) to north and Woton's Throne (7,721 ft/2,353 m) to the northeast. These peaks are also visible from Cape Royal.

Just ahead at mile 18 (km 29) are **Walhalla Overlook** and the ruin of **Walhalla Glades Pueblo,** which was occupied for about 100 years (about AD 1050–1150) by seasonal farmers from the **Unkar Delta** inside the canyon. A great red deposit at the confluence of Unkar Creek and the Colorado River, the Unkar Delta was populated and farmed from about AD 850–1200 and is visible from Walhalla Overlook. In the visitor center there's a pamphlet describing a self-guided tour of the ruin across the road.

To see where the farmers of Walhalla Glades likely obtained some of their water, stop at mile 19.1 (km 31) and take the approximately 1-mile (1.6-km) round-trip trail into the forest to **Cliff Spring.**

Finally, at mile 19.7 (km 32), you come to **Cape Royal,** a wonderful terminus with breathtaking views of the Colorado River and across the canyon to the South Rim, reached by an easy, paved trail (about 1 mi/1.6 km round-trip) lined with cliffrose, wind-sculpted pinyons and junipers, and random multicolored boulders. Along the trail you'll pass the rock arch **Angels Window,** which offers a perfectly framed view of the river.

Drive back to the lodge via the same road, and don't forget to stop at Point Imperial if you didn't already.

POINT SUBLIME DRIVE

DRIVING DISTANCE: 17.7 miles (28.5 km) one-way
DRIVING TIME: 2 hours-half a day
START: Point Sublime Road, 2.7 miles (4.3 km) North of Grand Canyon Lodge off AZ-67
END: Point Sublime Road, 2.7 miles (4.3 km) North of Grand Canyon Lodge off AZ-67

Point Sublime is a hard-won viewpoint—some say the best on either rim—with 200-degree views of the canyon from a jutting rock promontory at the end of about 18 miles (29 km) of rough, rocky, narrow dirt road. It is not to be trifled with in a regular passenger car—especially not a rental! The **Point Sublime Road** is for high-clearance SUVs, Jeeps, Subarus, and trucks only (plus mountain bikes, of course).

For most of its length the road is one lane and hemmed in hard by overgrowth on either side. There are a few places where you run the risk of getting an "Arizona paint job," with the brush scratching the sides of your rig as you pass. The road winds west across the plateau through a stretch of wonderful old-growth forest—ponderosa pine, quaking aspen, spruce fir evergreens, fallen trees, and burned areas covered in wildflowers.

Expect the drive to take at least an hour one-way, with a few stops along the way. Figure on spending half the day on this trip, better the first half; sunset out here is amazing,

Point Sublime

but driving back in the dark could be dangerous. You can camp at primitive sites with a permit from the **North Rim Backcountry Information Center** (North Rim Administration Bldg., 8am-noon and 1pm-5pm daily May 15-Oct. 15).

The Grand Canyon comes into view about two-thirds of the way in, and there's a small pullout and short path to an overlook. As you come up to the main attraction, **Point Sublime,** the vegetation changes quite suddenly to wind-sculpted pinyon-juniper and desert scrub.

Follow the short path out to the promontory. There are picnic tables near the parking lot at the end of the road.

To reach the Point Sublime Road, take AZ 67 north from the lodge 2.7 miles (4.3 km) and turn left (west).

Before you head out, check the most current road conditions with a ranger at the North Rim Visitor Center or the North Rim Backcountry Information Center. Also, take plenty of water and food and warm clothing, as well as tools and other backcountry-driving supplies.

BEST HIKES

TRANSEPT TRAIL
DISTANCE: 3 miles (4.8 km) round-trip
DURATION: 1.5 hours
ELEVATION GAIN: 200 feet (61 m)
EFFORT: Easy
TRAIL CONDITIONS: Mostly flat and hard-packed dirt, some sand and dust
TRAILHEADS: Grand Canyon Lodge or North Rim Campground

The Transept Trail leads north from behind Grand Canyon Lodge along the forested rim of the **Transept,** a deep side canyon southwest of the lodge, and ends in the woods just beyond the North Rim Campground. It's a useful trail if you're staying at the campground and don't want to use your car every time you go to the lodge area. This is also a good trail to take if you are going to the general store from the lodge area. Even if you're not staying at the campground or going to the store, this trail is worth walking to see the canyon from different points along

the rim and to spend some time in the oak-and-pine forest.

There are benches along the trail for resting and staring, and it's a good spot, especially early in the morning, for seeing small groups of grazing deer, busy squirrels running up and down the pine trees, and maybe even a prissy and hurried wild turkey with a line of chicks following close behind. Don't miss the small **Ancestral Puebloan ruin** along this trail about midway to the campground, once a two-room home for seasonal farmers. This trail can be made into a 3.6-mile (5.8-km) loop by taking the **Bridle Trail** back to the lodge area.

POINT IMPERIAL TRAIL
DISTANCE: 4.4 miles (7.1 km) round-trip
DURATION: 2 hours
ELEVATION GAIN: Negligible
EFFORT: Easy
TRAIL CONDITIONS: Dirt, some rocks and overgrowth
TRAILHEAD: Point Imperial parking lot, 5.4 miles (8.7 km) up Cape Royal Road

A primarily flat and easy trail, this route leads through a large wildfire-altered landscape that's exploding with new life, sprouting young aspens and pines here at the highest point on the North Rim. This out-and-back trail provides an interesting perspective on the long cycle of destruction and creation that rules the Southwest's highland forests. This is the **Saddle Mountain** area, the eastern edge of the plateau, with excellent views of **Marble Canyon** and **Navajo Mountain.** The turn-around point is a gate that marks the park's northern edge about 2.2 miles (3.5 km) in.

CAPE FINAL TRAIL

DISTANCE: 4.2 miles (6.8 km) round-trip
DURATION: 2 hours
ELEVATION GAIN: 150 feet (46 m)
EFFORT: Easy
TRAIL CONDITIONS: Old dirt road with a few rocks
TRAILHEAD: Dirt parking lot at mile 17.2 (km 27.7) on Cape Royal Road, about 3 miles (4.8 km) from Cape Royal

Geologist Clarence Dutton, whose love of grandeur and ancient world religions can be discerned in nearly every Grand Canyon landmark he named, gave Cape Final its rather peremptory title in 1882 after riding his horse out to the promontory and declaring it "doubtless the most interesting spot on the Kaibab." You can judge for yourself by hiking this easy trail through the pine trees, green brush, and burned spots to a promontory on the Walhalla Plateau with views of **Unkar Creek, Painted Desert,** and **Freya Castle.**

Transept Trail (top); Point Imperial (middle); Cape Final (bottom)

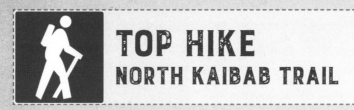

TOP HIKE
NORTH KAIBAB TRAIL

DISTANCE: 1.5-9.4 miles (2.4-15.1 km) round-trip
DURATION: 2-8 hours
ELEVATION GAIN: 3,050 feet (930 m) from trailhead to Roaring Springs
EFFORT: Moderate to very strenuous
TRAIL CONDITIONS: Rocky, sandy in places, mule leavings on upper sections, dusty and technical in parts
TRAILHEAD: 1.5 miles (2.4 km) north of Grand Canyon Lodge on east side of AZ 67

The North Kaibab Trail starts out among the coniferous heights of the North Rim. The forest surrounding the trail soon dries out and becomes a red-rock desert, the trail cut into the rock face of the cliffs and twisting down improbable routes hard against the cliffs, with nothing but your sanity keeping you away from the gorge. This is the only patrolled North Rim route down into the inner canyon and to the Colorado River. Sooner than you realize, the walls close in, and you are deep in the canyon, the trees on the rim just green blurs now.

A good introduction to this corridor trail and ancient native route is the short, 1.5-mile (2.4-km) round-trip jog down to the **Coconino Overlook,** from which, on a clear day, you can see the San Francisco Peaks and the South Rim. A 4-mile (6.4-km) round-trip hike down will get you to **Supai Tunnel,** opened up out of the red rock in the 1930s by the Civilian Conservation Corps. A little more than a mile (1.6 km) onward you'll reach **The Bridge in the Redwall** (5.2 mi/8.4 km round-trip), built in 1966 after a flood ruined this portion of the trail.

For a tough, all-day hike that will likely have you sore but smiling the next morning, take the North Kaibab roughly 5 miles (8 km) down to **Roaring Springs,** the source of life-giving Bright Angel Creek. The springs fall headlong out of the cliffside and spray mist and rainbows into the hot air. Just remember, you also have to go 5 miles (8 km) back up.

Start hiking as early as you can no matter what the season. In the summer it's not even debatable. You may be on the North Rim, but it's still dangerously hot inside the canyon. Try to be out and done by 10am during the hot months. Though not as important from a safety perspective in spring and early fall, an early start will put you ahead of the crowds and make it more likely to see wildlife along the trail.

The trailhead has a decent-sized parking lot, though it fills up during the high season, so the earlier you get here the better. You can also arrange for a shuttle from Grand Canyon Lodge, or walk 1.5 miles (2.4 km) from the lodge to the trailhead via the Bridle Trail.

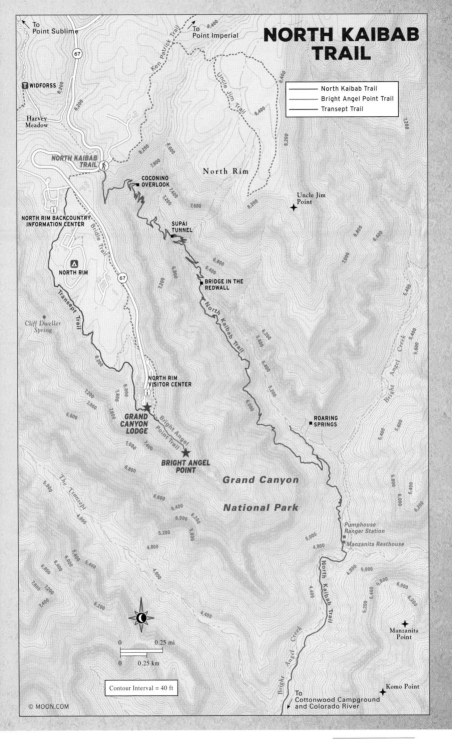

NORTH KAIBAB TRAIL

To
Point Sublime

To
Point Imperial

Ken Patrick Trail

Uncle Jim Trail

67

WIDFORSS

8,200

8,400

8,400

8,200

7,200

Legend:
North Kaibab Trail
Bright Angel Point Trail
Transept Trail

Harvey
Meadow

North Rim

Uncle Jim
Point

NORTH KAIBAB
TRAIL

7,800

8,000

7,600

COCONINO
OVERLOOK

6,800

NORTH RIM BACKCOUNTRY
INFORMATION CENTER

Bridle Trail

SUPAI
TUNNEL

7,200

6,800

6,400

NORTH RIM

67

6,800

BRIDGE IN THE
REDWALL

North Kaibab Trail

6,400

6,000

5,200

5,400

5,600

6,000

6,400

6,800

7,000

Bright Angel Creek

Transept Trail

Cliff Dweller
Spring

7,200

1,800

7,600

8,200

NORTH RIM
VISITOR CENTER

7,200
7,000
7,600

GRAND
CANYON
LODGE

6,800

7,000

7,400

Bright Angel Point Trail

BRIGHT ANGEL
POINT

ROARING
SPRINGS

5,400

5,600

5,800

6,000

6,400

6,200

The Transept

6,800

6,600

6,400

6,000

5,200

5,600

6,200

Grand Canyon

National Park

Pumphouse
Ranger Station
Manzanita Resthouse

5,000

4,800

4,800

5,000

North Kaibab Trail

4,400

5,200

5,400

5,800

6,000

5,000

4,600

5,400

5,000

5,400

4,800

4,600

4,600

7,000
7,200
7,400

6,200

4,400

Manzanita
Point

0   0.25 mi

0   0.25 km

Contour Interval = 40 ft

Bright Angel Creek

Komo Point

To
Cottonwood Campground
and Colorado River

© MOON.COM

Widforss Trail (left); Cliff Spring Trail (right)

CLIFF SPRING TRAIL

DISTANCE: 1 mile (1.6 km) round-trip
DURATION: 1 hour
ELEVATION GAIN: 150 feet (46 m)
EFFORT: Easy
TRAIL CONDITIONS: Rocky, steep, narrow
TRAILHEAD: Across the road from a small pullout at mile 19.1 (km 30.7) on Cape Royal Road, 0.3 mile (0.5 km) from Cape Royal

Take this short trail downhill into the forest of pine, oak, and aspen, away from the rim, to one of the many North Rim springs seeping and trickling out a shady overhang of Kaibab limestone. Like Dripping Spring down the South Rim's Hermit Trail, just a trickle of water creates a relatively lush microclimate here, surely one of the reasons why Ancestral Puebloan farmers lived nearby and built a **granary** along the trail, the ruins of which can be seen about 100 yards (91 m) from the trailhead. Don't drink the water without treating it first.

WIDFORSS TRAIL

DISTANCE: 10 miles (16.1 km) round-trip
DURATION: 4-6 hours
ELEVATION GAIN: 1,000 feet (305 m)
EFFORT: Easy to moderate
TRAIL CONDITIONS: Packed dirt, sometimes rocky, dusty, undulating
TRAILHEAD: From Grand Canyon Lodge, drive north on AZ 67 for 2.7 miles (4.3 km), turn left (west) onto a dirt road (Point Sublime Road), and follow signs to trailhead.

Named for the 1920s-1930s canyon painter Gunnar Widforss, the undulating, wildflower-lined Widforss Trail leads along the rim of Transept Canyon and through ponderosa pine, fir, and spruce forest, with a few stands of aspen and burned areas mixed in, for 5 miles (8 km) to **Widforss Point,** where you can stare across the great chasm and rest before heading back.

The trail starts out on the edge of **Harvey Meadow,** home to an early North Rim tourist camp. Across the meadow there's a cave with a doorway, which famed lion-killer Uncle Jim Owens used from time to time. Intermediate to expert hikers will have no problem hiking the entire 10-mile (16.1-km) round-trip route in less than four hours.

For a **shorter hike,** pick up the **free guide** to the Widforss Trail at the trailhead or the visitor center. It

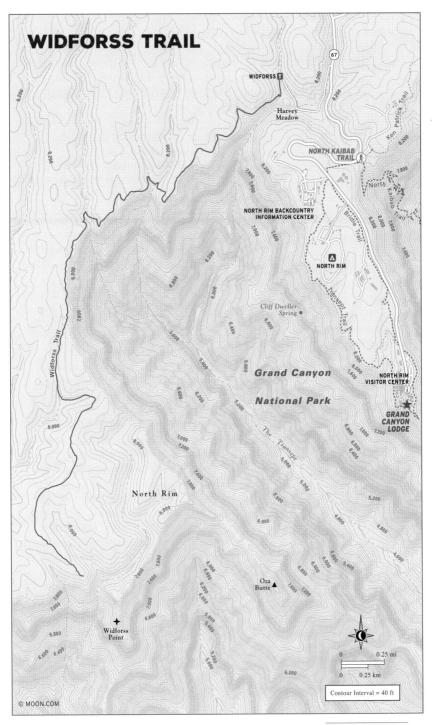

WIDFORSS TRAIL

WIDFORSS 🚻

67

Harvey
Meadow

NORTH KAIBAB
TRAIL 🚶

Ken Patrick Trail

North

NORTH RIM BACKCOUNTRY
INFORMATION CENTER

Bridle Trail

North Kaibab Trail

🏕 NORTH RIM

Widforss Trail

Cliff Dweller
Spring ●

Transept Trail

Grand Canyon

National Park

NORTH RIM
VISITOR CENTER

The Transept

GRAND
CANYON
LODGE ★

North Rim

Oza
Butte ▲

Widforss
Point ✦

0   0.25 mi

0   0.25 km

Contour Interval = 40 ft

© MOON.COM

proposes a **5-mile (8-km) round-trip hike** on the first half of the trail (about 2-3 hours) and includes a map and information on the natural and human history of the North Rim.

There is no water available along this trail, so come prepared.

BACKPACKING

Backpacking into and through the canyon from the North Rim is not as popular as starting out from the South Rim. For all but the most highly experienced and prepared Grand Canyon backpackers, the North Kaibab Trail is the only viable route into the canyon from the North Rim. The Grand Canyon Lodge offers a **hiker shuttle** (daily May 15-Oct. 15, first person $7, each additional person $4) to the North Kaibab Trailhead, which leaves every morning from the lodge at 5:30am and 6am. Tickets must be purchased 24 hours in advance at the lodge.

PERMITS

All overnight trips below the rim require a backcountry permit from Grand Canyon National Park's **Backcountry Information Center** (928/638-7875, fax 928/638-2125; www.nps.gov/grca; grca_bic@nps.gov; $10 plus $8 pp per night). The earlier you apply for a permit the better; the earliest you can apply is 10 days before the first of the month four months before your proposed trip date.

NORTH KAIBAB TRAIL

DISTANCE: 28 miles (45 km) round-trip to Phantom Ranch and Colorado River
DURATION: 2-3 days or more
ELEVATION GAIN: 5,770 feet (1,759 m) to river
EFFORT: Strenuous to very strenuous

TRAIL CONDITIONS: Rocky, sandy, dusty, narrow, technical
TRAILHEAD: 1.5 miles (2.4 km) north of Grand Canyon Lodge on east side of AZ 67

Hiking the 14-mile (22.5-km) length of the North Kaibab Trail to the Colorado River is like walking southward from Canada to Mexico, beginning high up on the North Rim among the spruce, fir, and pine and ending at a cottonwood-shaded riparian oasis in a desert surrounded by high rock walls. It's an amazing and unforgettable journey, part of it on high and narrow cliffside paths blasted and carved into the Redwall, much of it within sight of life-giving **Bright Angel Creek** (which the trail crosses six times) as it falls across the hard land from Roaring Springs to its communion with the great river. You pass the wet greenery of **Roaring Springs** about 5 miles (8 km) from the rim, and just beyond is the old **Pumphouse Residence,** now a ranger station, and the **Manzanita Resthouse** near the creek, where there's seasonal drinking water and shade. At around the halfway point, 6.8 miles (10.9 km) from the rim, you reach the enchanting **Cottonwood Campground,** a creek-side campground and a great place to spend the night or even a couple of days exploring this less-visited end of the canyon. Another 2 miles (3.2 km) or so down the trail is **Ribbon Falls,** a

North Kaibab Trail

wonderful spot with falling water and moss and other shocking greenery on the dry red land. The final section of the trail before **Phantom Ranch, Bright Angel Campground,** and the **Colorado River** is a narrow stretch through the **inner gorge,** easy and flat but low and hot, boxed in by Vishnu schist about 1.7 billion years old. In the summer it's generally too hot to hike through the inner gorge after 10am.

There's drinking water available along the trail, but don't rely on it. May 15-October 14, you can refill your water bottle at the North Kaibab Trailhead, Supai Tunnel, Roaring Springs, Manzanita Rest Area, and Cottonwood Campground. All the water stations along the trail are turned off October 15-May 15. Always carry a water filter for use in Bright Angel Creek, which is close by for much of the hike.

ARIZONA TRAIL

DISTANCE: 12 miles (19.3 km) one-way
DURATION: 1-2 days
ELEVATION GAIN: Negligible
EFFORT: Moderate
TRAIL CONDITIONS: Dirt, rocky, sand in places
TRAILHEAD: Near North Kaibab Trail parking lot

A 12-mile (19.3-km) section of the monumental Arizona Trail, which traverses the state from south to north, starts at the North Kaibab Trail parking lot, winds and undulates through the thick plateau forest, and then ends at the boundary line of the Kaibab National Forest. To do the whole 12-mile (19.3-km) North

Rim section of the AZT, have someone drop you off at one end and pick you up at the other. The question then becomes which end to start at. If you're staying at the lodge or campground inside the park, start from the North Kaibab Trailhead parking lot, 1.5 miles (2.4 km) north of the lodge on AZ 67. The AZT trailhead is at the south end of the parking lot. The trail ends at a pull-out along Forest Road 610, about 5.5 miles (8.9 km) north of the park entrance station. If you're coming from Jacob Lake, start from the Forest Road 610 trailhead and end at the North Kaibab Trailhead parking lot. To reach the southern trailhead from Jacob Lake, take AZ 67 south for 26 miles (41.8 km), turn left on Forest Road 611, drive 1.1 miles (1.8 km) and turn right on Forest Road 610, then drive 5.1 miles (8.2 km) to a pullout. Look for the AZT trail sign. One way to do this trip is to hike into the park, stay the night in the campground, and then hike back the next day or two. This would require a reservation at the park campground.

From the North Kaibab Trail parking lot, the AZT crosses AZ 67, skirts Harvey Meadow and the Widforss Trailhead, runs north through the forest and winds back around to the North Rim Entrance Station and along the highway, and ends at the forest boundary. Leashed dogs and even bicycles are allowed on the trail (though make certain that you know for sure when the Arizona Trail ends and the North Kaibab begins—otherwise you'll have to contend with a ranger if you have a dog or a bike on the wrong one).

BIKING

BRIDLE TRAIL

3 mi (4.8 km) round-trip

The Bridle Trail is a useful trail for exploring the park or just getting from one place to another. The trail of hard-packed dirt is open to walkers, bicycles, and dogs on leashes—the only trail in the North Rim section of the park that allows pets and bikes. It runs for about 1.5 miles (2.4 km) through tall pines, passing all the main park buildings and paralleling AZ 67 all the way to the **North Kaibab Trailhead.** This trail can get busy, and with the bikes and dogs added into the mix it requires heads-up hiking at all times. One of the best ways to use this trail if you are staying at the campground is to bring your bikes along and ride it back and forth from the lodge complex to your campsite.

POINT SUBLIME ROAD

17.7 mi (28.5 km) one-way

The rugged Point Sublime Road inside the park is also a popular mountain bike ride. It's a 4-wheel-drive road, fun to negotiate on a mountain bike and ending at one of the most jaw-dropping viewpoints on the rim. Watch for cars along the way as it's a popular route for Jeeps and trucks. There are a few monster hills, and it's all pretty rocky and also sandy in some spots.

RENTALS

There are no bike rentals available on the North Rim. Bring your mountain bikes with you. For information about trails, stop by the **Kaibab Plateau Visitor Center** (928/643-7298; www.fs.usda.gov; 8am-5pm daily mid-May-mid-Oct.) in Jacob Lake or the **North Rim Country Store** (AZ 67, mile marker 605, 18 mi/29 km north of the rim; 928/638-2383; www.northrimcountrystore.com; 7am-7pm daily mid-May-late Oct.) along AZ 67.

Bridle Trail

NORTH RIM FOOD OPTIONS

NAME	LOCATION	TYPE
★ Grand Canyon Lodge Dining Room	Grand Canyon Lodge	sit-down restaurant
Deli in the Pines	Grand Canyon Lodge	casual and take-out
Coffee Shop / Roughrider Saloon	next to Grand Canyon Lodge	coffee shop/bar

FOOD

The dining options on the North Rim are few and far apart, with only three full-service restaurants on the Kaibab Plateau to choose from. If you are on a tight budget, have a lot of dietary restrictions or food allergies, or just like to make your own dinner, consider filling a cooler with foodstuffs before you ascend the plateau. Most of the cabins and rooms at the Grand Canyon Lodge come with small refrigerators, and some of the cabins at Kaibab Lodge have refrigerators and microwave ovens. You can also find groceries, though not a lot of fresh fruits and vegetables, at the general store inside the park or at the North Rim Country Store, about 18 miles (29 km) north of the lodge on AZ 67. If you are only going to eat at one restaurant, make it the Grand Canyon Lodge Dining Room. The atmosphere, the views, and the history—not to mention the excellent, regionally sourced food—make for an enchanting dining experience.

STANDOUTS
Grand Canyon Lodge Dining Room
928/638-8560; gnrfbmgr@gcnr.com
With its native stone walls and picture windows framing the impossible vastness of the canyon, the Grand Canyon Lodge Dining Room must be seen even if you don't eat here. Its high ceilings, wrought-iron chandeliers, Native American symbols, and exposed wood rafters give this large, bright, and open space an unforgettable atmosphere and represent the height of the National Park Service Rustic style. All the dining options at Grand Canyon Lodge are closed from mid-October to mid-May. To make reservations for spring, summer, or fall while the lodge and restaurants are closed, call Forever Resorts (877/386-4383).

The restaurant is a member of the Green Restaurant Association and serves dishes with a touch of regional and national park history made from fresh, organic, and

FOOD	PRICE	HOURS
American	moderate	6:30am-10am, 11:30am-2:30pm, 4:30pm-9:30pm daily mid-May-mid-Oct.
deli food	budget	10:30am-9pm daily mid-May-mid-Oct.
breakfast/bar snacks	budget	coffee shop 5:30am-11am daily mid-May-mid-Oct.; bar 11am-11pm daily mid-May-mid-Oct.

sustainable produce, meat, chicken, and fish. Breakfast (6:30am-10am daily; $6.70-17.50; buffet $17.50 adults, $9.25 children) features all the hearty and healthy classics (yogurt, oatmeal, etc.) plus Arizona favorites like tamales and eggs, and huevos rancheros. Vegetarians will like the grilled vegetable wrap and the braised portobello on offer at lunch (11:30am-2:30pm daily; $6.20-19.50), and everybody will love the fantastic soup, salad, and sandwich buffet ($17.50 adults, $9.25 children). For dinner (4:30pm-9:30pm daily; $11.35-33.95; reservations highly recommended), choose between the Bright Angel Buffet with prime rib (4:30pm-6:30pm daily; $32.95 adults, $18.95 children) and a menu featuring fresh fish, grilled veggie kababs, pasta, steaks, and bison burgers.

BEST PICNIC SPOTS
Grand Canyon Lodge Veranda
Southern Terminus of AZ 67, out the back door of the lodge

If you find one of the many

Grand Canyon Lodge Veranda (left); Point Imperial Picnic Area (right)

NORTH RIM CAMPGROUNDS

NAME	LOCATION	SEASON
North Rim	Grand Canyon Lodge area	mid-May–mid-Oct. (primitive camping Dec.–mid-May)

Adirondack chairs facing the Grand Canyon on the lodge's back porch unoccupied, you've lucked into one of the best al fresco dining areas in the park. Only simple fare will work here—sandwiches, breakfast burritos, etc.—and there's not a lot of elbow room, but the view and ambiance cannot be matched. In the evening grab a beer or glass of wine at the Roughrider Saloon near the lodge's front entrance before heading out to the porch to watch the sunset.

Point Imperial Picnic Area
Point Imperial, 11 miles (17.7 km) from visitor center

There's something special about eating at 8,803 feet (2,683 m) above sea level, at the very highest point in Grand Canyon National Park. Point Imperial Picnic Area and viewpoint is a breezy rim-side spot with expansive and varied views to the east—Navajoland, Painted Desert, and Marble Canyon—and in the foreground, Mount Hayden, an 8,372-foot (2,552-m) rock peak from which it's hard to turn your gaze. There are a few picnic tables and benches here, along with a vault toilet and trash cans.

To get here, take AZ 67 north from the visitor center, at mile 3 (km 4.8) turn right onto Cape Royal Road, and then at mile 5.4 (km 8.7) veer left to Point Imperial.

Cape Royal Picnic Area
Southern Terminus of Cape Royal Road, 23 miles (73 km) from visitor center

At the end of the Cape Royal Road waits the improbable hole-in-a-rock called Angels Window, with its magical glimpse of the Colorado River falling and rolling through the canyon. There are several shaded off-trail spots for a ground-level picnic (there are a few benches, but no tables after the parking lot) along the paved route, which ends at Cape Royal, an amazing viewpoint and the last stop on the Cape Royal Drive. At the trailhead there's a large gravel parking area with a few picnic tables, vault toilets, and trash cans.

SITES AND AMENITIES	RV LIMIT	PRICE	RESERVATIONS
75 tent and RV sites, 12 tent-only sites; flush and composting toilets; potable water; no showers or hookups	27 ft (8.2 m)	$18-25	yes, required mid-May-Oct. (recreation.gov)

CAMPING

Reservations

The campground on the North Rim is open with full services from mid-May to mid-October, and you must reserve a spot in advance. For the park and national forest campgrounds, individual sites are "released" for reservations six months ahead of time on www.recreation.gov (so if your preferred date is, say, July 15, you must reserve a site, if you can, on January 15 starting at 8am MST).

Tips

Even summer nights on the plateau can be chilly, so pack accordingly.

North Rim Campground

NORTH RIM LODGING

NAME	LOCATION
★ Grand Canyon Lodge	Grand Canyon Lodge

LODGING

STANDOUTS
★ Grand Canyon Lodge
877/386-4383; www.grandcanyon-forever.com; mid-May-mid-Oct.

The historic Grand Canyon Lodge rises from the North Rim at the end of AZ 67, a rustic masterpiece of local sandstone and pine gloriously isolated at 8,000 feet (2,438 m) on what feels like the very edge of the known world. The main lodge building hangs rim-side above Bright Angel Point, the bottom of a U-shaped complex connected by porticos, and it houses the reception desk, the bright and high-ceilinged dining room, and the enchanting sunroom with its huge picture windows overlooking the canyon. Even if you aren't staying here, spend some time in the sunroom and on the lodge's terrace, both of which are essential North Rim experiences.

Cabins of various sizes dot the forest north, east, and west of the lodge, along with two large outbuildings with motel-style rooms. The motel rooms ($148 per night)

Grand Canyon Lodge

SEASON	OPTIONS	PRICE
mid-May–mid-Oct.	motel rooms and cabins	motel rooms starting at $148; cabins starting at $163

are charming and comfortable, and some have connecting doors useful for families, but the cabins—including some with incredible views of the canyon—are the lodge's main draw. The stone-and-pine cabins all have private bathrooms and romantic stone fireplaces that have been converted to gas. Staying in one can make you feel like a wilderness wanderer bedded down in rare comfort. They come in three sizes: the small and basic Frontier Cabin ($163); the two-room Pioneer Cabin, which sleeps up to six ($188-191); and the larger Western Cabin ($262-301) with two queen beds and a front porch with rough-hewn rocking chairs. There are mini-fridges and coffeemakers in most of the rooms and cabins, and kids under 15 stay free (though it's an extra $15 per night if you want a rollaway bed, which are not allowed in the Frontier Cabins).

Grand Canyon Lodge cabins

INFORMATION AND SERVICES

Entrance Stations

North Rim Entrance

AZ 67

The lone North Rim Entrance Station to Grand Canyon National Park stands along AZ 67 about 30 miles (48 km) south of Jacob Lake and the U.S.89A junction. After you pay your entrance fee, a ranger will give you a free copy of the *North Rim Pocket Map & Services Guide,* which is a valuable reference for exploring the park. If you plan to arrive outside of regular hours, you can buy a pass at www.recreation.gov and download the guide at www.nps.gov/grca, or there is a self-pay station at the visitor center where you can also pick up a free guide. From here it's another 14 miles (22.5 km) to the rim and the stately Grand Canyon Lodge and most of the park's services. AZ 67, a beautiful stretch of blacktop running through a forest mixed with evergreens, fire-blackened husks, white aspens, and green meadows, is the only road into and out of the park.

Visitor Centers

North Rim Visitor Center

8am-6pm daily May 15-Oct. 16, 9am-3pm daily Oct. 17-30

The North Rim Visitor Center is next to Grand Canyon Lodge and is staffed with several rangers and volunteers who can direct you to the best sights and trails. Here you'll find fascinating exhibits on canyon science and lore, as well as a bathroom and water station. Within the visitor center the nonprofit Grand Canyon Conservancy operates an excellent bookstore with all the essential tomes and other media about Grand Canyon and the Great Southwest. This is where you go to find out the current ranger programs on offer and to bombard a hard-working ranger with all your questions about the canyon and the park.

TRANSPORTATION

Getting There

A road trip to Grand Canyon's North Rim is not to be taken lightly. The Kaibab Plateau is an isolated highland country crisscrossed by rough forest roads that is sparsely populated and dormant for half the year. A road-ready vehicle is essential. Take along extra water, food, and supplies even if you're staying in one of the three hotels on the plateau; being overprepared is better than the alternative.

There is only one way into Grand Canyon National Park's North Rim section—U.S. 89A to AZ 67, a paved (only since 1941) two-lane through the forest that ends at the rim and is one of the most scenic and thrilling roads in Arizona. While driving on the plateau, keep an eye out for motorcycles, which proliferate during the summer, and for cyclists riding on the nonexistent shoulder. Also keep a watch out for wildlife, including elk, deer, turkeys, and all sorts of other scurrying furry creatures that pay little heed to the highway.

The many Forest Service roads around the Kaibab Plateau are mostly dirt or gravel and should be taken on a case-by-case basis; some should be avoided unless you have a high-profile vehicle. In July, August, and September, expect daily late-afternoon thunderstorms that can quickly wash out a road or create a flash flood. To reach some of the backpacking trails here, you will need a high-profile vehicle or even a four-wheel drive. If you don't have one of these, and especially if you are driving a rental car, consider trying a trail that's easier to access.

From the North Rim Entrance

The North Rim has only one entrance station; it's about 30 miles (48.2 km) south of

Jacob Lake along **AZ 67.** After you enter the park, stay on AZ 67 south for 14 miles (22.5 km), about 25 minutes, to reach the North Rim Visitor Center and Grand Canyon Lodge.

From the South Rim

The North Rim is 210 miles (338 km) from the South Rim, and the drive typically takes about four hours. Leave the South Rim through the East Entrance in Desert View, which is about 22 miles (35.4 km) from the Grand Canyon Visitor Center along **AZ 64.** After leaving the park, follow AZ 64 to Cameron, on the Navajo Nation, where you'll pick up **U.S. 89.** Drive 57 miles (91.7 km) north from Cameron to Bitter Springs and pick up **U.S. 89A,** crossing the Colorado River at Navajo Bridge and the lonely Arizona Strip to Jacob Lake, about 56 miles (90.1 km). At Jacob Lake pick up **AZ 67** and drive 44 miles (70.8 km) to the North Rim Visitor Center and Grand Canyon Lodge.

From Grand Canyon West

It's a long, 6.5-hour drive from Grand Canyon West to the North Rim, much of it through Nevada and Utah rather than Arizona. From Grand Canyon West take **Pierce Ferry Road** to **US 93** at Dolan Springs, about 58 miles (93.3 km). Follow US 93, **I-11, I-15,** and **UT-9/59** for 204 miles (328.3 km), reentering Arizona at Colorado City and picking up **AZ 389** to **US 89A** to **AZ-67,** and the North Rim another 137 miles (220.5 km).

Shuttles

Trans-Canyon Shuttle

928/638-2820; www.trans-canyon-shuttle.com; $90 one-way; reservations required
While you really need your own vehicle to do the North Rim right, for hikers the Trans-Canyon Shuttle is also a good option. Rim-to-rim hikers starting on the North Kaibab Trail can take the shuttle to the North Rim after leaving a car on the South Rim for when they finally ascend from the depths. Or, they can start from the South Rim via the Bright Angel or South Kaibab Trail and then ride the shuttle back to the South Rim and their car. Of course the plan also would work if they left a car on the North Rim and then took the shuttle back from the South Rim. For most visitors, though, it's better to end a rim-to-rim hike on the South Rim, as it is much closer to Sky Harbor Airport in Phoenix. During the high season (spring and summer), shuttles run twice daily from the South Rim to the North Rim (8am-12:30pm and 1:30pm-6pm) and twice daily from the North Rim to the South Rim (7am-11:30am and 2pm-6:30pm). The 215-mile (345-km) drive—through the Navajo Reservation, across the Colorado River at Marble Canyon, onto the lonely bunchgrass plains of the Arizona Strip, and then twisting up to the high forested Kaibab Plateau—takes about 4.5 hours.

Parking

Inside the park there's parking at the lodge and the campground. On any given summer day, especially on a weekend, parking can be a challenge. However, patience and a willingness to walk a good distance are generally rewarded. There's a decent-sized parking lot at the North Kaibab Trailhead north of the lodge, but it generally fills up during the high season, so the earlier you start your hike into the gorge the more likely you are to find a parking spot.

Gas

There are only three gas stations on the plateau: Jacob Lake, about 45 miles (72 km) from the rim; the North Rim Country Store, on AZ 67 about 18 miles (29 km) north of the rim; and inside the park.

Indian Garden

THE INNER CANYON

Inside the canyon is a strange desert, red and green, pink and rocky. It's those sheer rock walls, tight and claustrophobic in the interior's narrowest slots, that make this place a different world altogether. A large part of a canyon-crossing hike along the corridor trails takes place in Bright Angel Canyon along Bright Angel Creek. As you hike along the trail beside the creek, greenery and the cool rushing water clash with the silent heat washing off the cliffs.

On any given night there are only a few hundred visitors sleeping below the rim—at Phantom Ranch, a Mary Jane Colter-designed lodge near the mouth of Bright Angel Canyon; at three campgrounds along the corridor trails; or off in the canyon's wild backcountry. Until a few decades ago visiting the inner canyon was something of a free-for-all, but these days access to the interior is strictly controlled; you have to purchase a permit, and they're not always easy to get—each year the park receives about 30,000 requests for backcountry permits and issues only 13,000.

No matter which trail you use, there's no avoiding an arduous, leg- and spirit-punishing hike there and back if you really want to see the inner canyon. It's not easy, no matter who you are, but it is worth it; it's a true accomplishment, a hard walk you'll never forget.

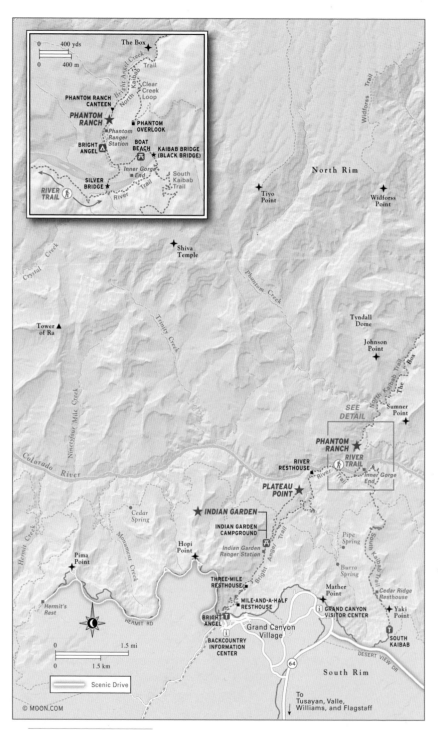

The Box

400 yds

400 m

PHANTOM RANCH CANTEEN

PHANTOM RANCH

Clear Creek Loop

PHANTOM OVERLOOK

Phantom Ranger Station

BRIGHT ANGEL

BOAT BEACH

KAIBAB BRIDGE (BLACK BRIDGE)

Inner Gorge End

South Kaibab Trail

SILVER BRIDGE

RIVER TRAIL

North Rim

Tiyo Point

Widforss Point

Shiva Temple

Phantom Creek

Tyndall Dome

Johnson Point

Tower of Ra

Trinity Creek

The Box

SEE DETAIL

Sumner Point

PHANTOM RANCH

RIVER TRAIL

Colorado River

River Resthouse

Inner Gorge End

PLATEAU POINT

INDIAN GARDEN

INDIAN GARDEN CAMPGROUND

Pipe Spring

Cedar Spring

Indian Garden Ranger Station

Hopi Point

Burro Spring

Pima Point

THREE-MILE RESTHOUSE

Mather Point

Cedar Ridge Resthouse

Hermit's Rest

MILE-AND-A-HALF RESTHOUSE

BRIGHT ANGEL

GRAND CANYON VISITOR CENTER

Yaki Point

HERMIT RD

Grand Canyon Village

SOUTH KAIBAB

BACKCOUNTRY INFORMATION CENTER

DESERT VIEW DR

1.5 mi

64

1.5 km

South Rim

Scenic Drive

© MOON.COM

To Tusayan, Valle, Williams, and Flagstaff

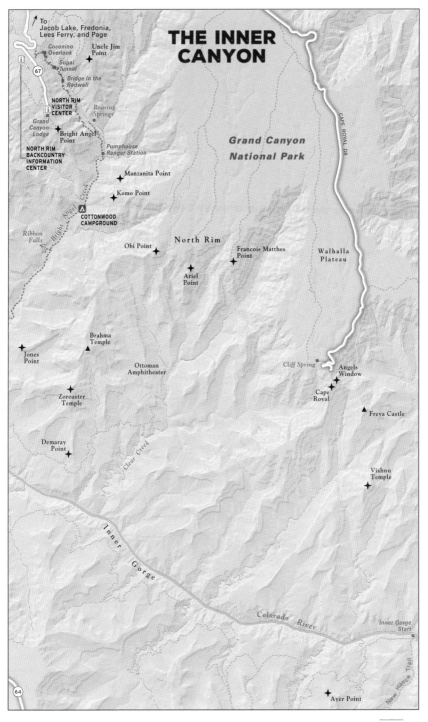

THE INNER CANYON

To Jacob Lake, Fredonia, Lees Ferry, and Page

67

Coconino Overlook
Supai Tunnel
Bridge in the Redwall
Uncle Jim Point

NORTH RIM VISITOR CENTER

Roaring Springs

Grand Canyon Lodge

Bright Angel Point

NORTH RIM BACKCOUNTRY INFORMATION CENTER

Pumphouse Ranger Station

Grand Canyon National Park

CAPE ROYAL DR

Manzanita Point

Komo Point

Bright Angel Creek

COTTONWOOD CAMPGROUND

Ribbon Falls

Obi Point

North Rim

Walhalla Plateau

Francois Matthes Point

Ariel Point

Jones Point

Brahma Temple

Ottoman Amphitheater

Cliff Spring

Angels Window

Cape Royal

Zoroaster Temple

Freya Castle

Demaray Point

Clear Creek

Vishnu Temple

Inner Gorge

Colorado River

Inner Gorge Start

64

New Hance Trail

Ayer Point

2

TOP 3

★ **1. INDIAN GARDEN:** Stop at this spring-fed oasis on the Bright Angel Trail, where you can rest below the tall cottonwoods and watch wildlife flit through the greenery (page 134).

★ **2. PLATEAU POINT:** Look down on the roiling Colorado River from this amazing cliff-edge viewpoint (page 135).

★ **3. PHANTOM RANCH:** Stay overnight at the wonderful green heart of the inner canyon (page 151).

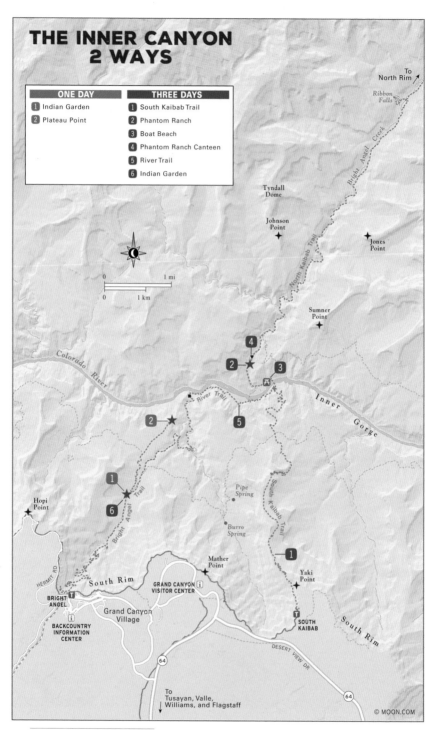

THE INNER CANYON 2 WAYS

ONE DAY
1. Indian Garden
2. Plateau Point

THREE DAYS
1. South Kaibab Trail
2. Phantom Ranch
3. Boat Beach
4. Phantom Ranch Canteen
5. River Trail
6. Indian Garden

To North Rim

Ribbon Falls

Bright Angel Creek

Tyndall Dome

Johnson Point

Jones Point

North Kaibab Trail

Sumner Point

Colorado River

4

2

3

River Trail

5

Inner Gorge

2

Pipe Spring

South Kaibab Trail

1

6

Bright Angel Trail

Hopi Point

Burro Spring

Mather Point

Yaki Point

South Rim

HERMIT RD

BRIGHT ANGEL

GRAND CANYON VISITOR CENTER

BACKCOUNTRY INFORMATION CENTER

Grand Canyon Village

SOUTH KAIBAB

South Rim

DESERT VIEW DR

64

To Tusayan, Valle, Williams, and Flagstaff

64

© MOON.COM

INNER CANYON 2 WAYS

ONE DAY

1   Hike the Bright Angel Trail from the South Rim to **Indian Garden,** and turn back here for a 9.6-mile (15.4-km) round-trip hike. Otherwise, if you're ambitious...

2   Go all the way to **Plateau Point** (another 3 mi/4.8 km round-trip from Indian Garden) to catch a glimpse of the Colorado River. Note: Do not attempt this in summer unless you get a very early start.

THREE DAYS

This multi-day backpacking trip (starting and ending on the South Rim) requires permits and reservations (you must apply for a permit six months prior to your planned hike date).

1 Hike down the **South Kaibab Trail,** a steep and sun-exposed trail that's the fastest way to the river (7.4 mi/11.9 km one-way), descending some 4,860 feet (1,481 m) from its trailhead at Yaki Point and offering amazing views of the canyon.

2 When you reach **Phantom Ranch,** hang out at the riverside, meeting fellow backpackers from all over the world, and dip your tired feet in Bright Angel Creek.

3 If you're up for a bit more exercise, walk over to **Boat Beach** and watch the river-trippers floating by.

4 Kick back with a beer or two at the **Phantom Ranch Canteen** before turning in for the night.

5 On the second day of your trip, day-hike along the **River Trail,** keeping your eyes out for friendly desert big-horn sheep and other wildlife as you surrender to the deep canyon and its magical atmosphere.

6 On your hike-out day, get an early start and take the Bright Angel Trail out to the South Rim, stopping at **Indian Garden** for a picnic lunch.

3

AVOID THE CROWDS

While the Grand Canyon is incredibly vast, and while only a tiny portion of the millions of Grand Canyon National Park visitors find their way to the inner canyon, there are only three small campgrounds and one small lodge along the corridor trails between the South and North Rims. During the busy spring and fall seasons, you may find yourself not exactly in a crowd, but perhaps among a few more people than you had hoped for. To avoid such "crowds" in the inner canyon, get up early and hit the **day-hiking routes around Phantom Ranch,** or consider launching your adventure in the winter, when it's cold and sometimes wet in the canyon, but not crowded at all.

More Ways to Avoid the Crowds

- Plateau Point
- River Trail
- Clear Creek Loop
- Phantom Ranch to Ribbon Falls

trail to Phantom Ranch

Ribbon Falls

INNER CANYON ROUTES

Although there are many lesser-known routes into and through the canyon, most hikers stick to the **corridor trails—Bright Angel, South Kaibab,** and **North Kaibab.** (Recommended if you are new to Grand Canyon backpacking, even if you are an expert backpacker otherwise.)

SOUTH RIM: SOUTH KAIBAB AND BRIGHT ANGEL TRAILS

DISTANCE: 17.3 miles (27.8 km) round-trip
DURATION: 3 days
ELEVATION GAIN: 4,400-4,800 feet (1,300-1,500 m)
EFFORT: Moderate to strenuous
TRAIL CONDITIONS: Narrow, rocky, very steep, sandy in places; mule traffic, mule leavings
TRAILHEAD: Near Yaki Point on the East Rim
SHUTTLE STOP: Yaki Point, on Rim Route (Orange)

The standard backpacking trip into the canyon from the South Rim lasts three days. One day hiking in, one day inside the canyon, and one day hiking out. The trip starts on either the South Kaibab or the Bright Angel Trail and ends at **Bright Angel Campground** or **Phantom Ranch** in the inner gorge near the Colorado River. During the high season (Mar. 1-Nov. 14), you're allowed to spend up to two consecutive nights at Bright Angel or the other corridor campgrounds—Indian Garden Campground on the Bright Angel Trail and Cottonwood Campground on the North Kaibab Trail below the North Rim. (From Nov. 15-Feb. 28, the limit is four consecutive nights.)

Going in, it's best to take the **South Kaibab Trail**—it's very steep but dramatically beautiful and shorter than Bright Angel. You'll be inside the canyon kicking back under the cottonwoods along Bright Angel

Bright Angel Trail

Creek in no time. Going out, take the **Bright Angel Trail,** an arduous, punishing, and amazing hike out of the gorge, stopping for a rest at beautiful **Indian Garden.** For those who want to spend even more time inside the canyon, make a reservation to camp the third night at Indian Garden, and then hike out the rest of the way the next day. The **best times** to take this classic backpacking trip into the inner gorge are **March-April**

and **October-early November.** Avoid this area in the summer.

RIM TO RIM: BRIGHT ANGEL AND NORTH KAIBAB TRAILS

DISTANCE: 23.9 miles (38.5 km) round-trip
DURATION: 2-3 days
ELEVATION GAIN: North Kaibab Trail Elevation 5,781 feet (1,762 m); Bright Angel Trail 4,800 feet (1,463 m)
EFFORT: Moderate to strenuous
TRAIL CONDITIONS: Narrow, rocky, steep, sandy
TRAILHEAD: Just west of Bright Angel Lodge
SHUTTLE STOP: Bright Angel Lodge, on Village Route (Blue)

Rim-to-rim hikes are popular, though after October the **North Rim** is closed down and you may find yourself camping in snow at the North Rim Campground (and possibly even inside the canyon as well). While there are many athletes these days who like to rush through the canyon from rim-to-rim in one day, the truly magical part of a canyon backpacking trip is not so much the getting there but the being there. Spend as much time inside the canyon as you can; it takes a lot to get here, and it's a wonderous, unique place that should not be hurried through.

If you're set on a rim-to-rim hike with multiple days of camping below the rim, the **best times** to do it are in the early spring or the fall, **April or October**—but these are also some of the most difficult times to get permits. Summer, **May-September,** is **not a good time;** the canyon and the rims will be busy, and it will be 100-120°F (38-49°C) inside the canyon during the day and stay in the 80s (27-32°C) and 90s (32-37°C) once the sun goes down. Summer hiking in the canyon

Three-Mile Resthouse on Bright Angel Trail (top); North Kaibab Trail (bottom)

Bright Angel Trail

Phantom Ranch (left); mule trip (right)

should be done before 10am. During October high temperatures inside the canyon range 80-90°F (27-32°C), and then drop to the high 60s (19-21°C) and 70s (21-26°C) come November, making hiking much more pleasant than it is during the infernal summer months. High temperatures mostly stay around the 50s (10-15°C) and 60s (16-21°C) December-February, though nighttime temps in the canyon drop precipitously. In March expect inner canyon highs in the low 70s (21-23°C) and lows in the high 40s (8-9°C); in April typical highs warm up to the low 80s (27-29°C), with lows in the high 50s (13-15°C); and in early May expect highs in the low 90s (32-34°C) and lows in the low 60s (16-18°C).

At the end of your hike, you can ride the **Trans-Canyon Shuttle** (928/638-2820; www.trans-canyonshuttle.com; $90 one-way; reservations required) back to your car on the South Rim (or vice versa if starting on the North Rim). During the high season (spring and summer), shuttles run twice daily from the South Rim to the North Rim (8am-12:30pm and 1:30pm-6pm) and twice daily from the North Rim

to the South Rim (7am-11:30am and 2pm-6:30pm).

MULE TRIPS

For generations the famous Grand Canyon mules have been dexterously picking along the skinny trails, loaded with packs and people. Even the Brady Bunch rode them, so they come highly recommended. A descent into the canyon on the back of a friendly mule—with an often-taciturn cowboy-type leading the train—can be an unforgettable experience, but don't assume because you're riding and not walking that you won't be sore in the morning.

Park concessionaire **Xanterra** (888/297-2757; www.grandcanyonlodges.com) offers two mule trips to Phantom Ranch, a one-night excursion and a two-night expedition. The **one-night trip** is offered **year-round** and includes accommodations at Phantom Ranch (by booking a mule trip, you automatically reserve a spot at Phantom Ranch without having to enter the lottery), dinner and breakfast in the Phantom Ranch Canteen, and a sack

HIKING RIM TO RIM... THE EASY WAY

One of the first things you notice while journeying through the inner canyon is the advanced age of many of your fellow hikers. It is not uncommon to see men and women in their 70s and 80s hiking along at a good clip, packs on their backs and big smiles on their faces.

At the same time, all over the South Rim you'll see warning signs about overexertion, each featuring a buff young man in incredible shape suffering from heatstroke or exhaustion, with the warning that most of the people who die in the canyon—and people die every year—are people like him. You need not be a wilderness expert or marathon runner to enjoy even a long, 27-mile (43-km), rim-to-rim hike through the inner canyon. Don't let your fears hold you back from what is often a life-changing trip.

There are several strategies that can make a canyon hike much easier than a forced march with a 30-pound (13.6-kg) pack of gear on your back:

- Don't go in the summer; **wait until October or even November,** when it's cooler, though still quite warm, in the inner canyon.

- Try your best to **book a cabin or a dorm room at Phantom Ranch** rather than camping. That way, you'll need less equipment, you'll have all or most of your food taken care of, and there will be a shower and a beer waiting for you upon your arrival.

- For $76 each way, you can **hire a mule** to carry up to 30 pounds (13.6 kg) of gear for you, so all you have to bring is a daypack with water and snacks. This way, instead of suffering while you descend and ascend the trail, you'll be able to better enjoy the magnificence of this wonder of the world.

lunch. The cost for the one-night trip is $692.59 per person, $1,204.51 for two people, and $533.31 for each additional person. The **two-night trip** is offered **November–March** and includes accommodations at Phantom Ranch, meals in the canteen, and sack lunches. The cost for the two-night trip is $1,009.42 per person, $1,657.50 for two people, and $690.86 for each additional person. You can make a reservation up to 13 months in advance, and you really should do it as soon as you know your plans. There's a 225-pound (102-kg) weight restriction.

The mule trips begin in the stone corral next to the Bright Angel Lodge and descend into the canyon via the Bright Angel Trail, stopping for a box lunch at Indian Garden. The trips ascend from the inner gorge via the South Kaibab Trail. Expect to be in the saddle for about 5.5 hours each way. You are provided with a small plastic bag about the size of a 10-pound (4.5-kg) bag of ice to carry your toiletries and other items. If you need more luggage than this, you can send a duffel bag ahead for $76 each way (30 lb/13.6 kg maximum, 36 x 20 x 13 in/91 x 51 x 33 cm; www.grandcanyonlodges.com/lodging/phantom-ranch).

HIGHLIGHTS

★ INDIAN GARDEN

A beautiful oasis about 3,000 feet (914 m) below and 4.8 miles (7.7 km) from the South Rim, spring-fed Indian Garden entices hikers and backpackers down the twisting Bright Angel Trail, appearing as a thick line of green within an otherwise sharp and arid landscape from the bustling Grand Canyon Village high above. If you can handle a hard, steep, and mind-blowing 9.6 miles (15.4 km) round-trip (in spring and fall is best), a day hike to Indian Garden and back from the South Rim is one of the best things you can do in the national park.

In the desert Southwest, a little water makes all the difference, and the color green is all the more beautiful and inspiring because of its scarcity. So when you come across spring-fed oases like Indian Garden or riparian paradises such as Bright Angel Canyon, you stay awhile and celebrate. Indian Garden has been a place of human activity in the harsh inner canyon for at least 13,000 years. More recently, archaeological sites around the area date from the Ancestral Puebloans and Cohoninas, from about AD 300-1300, including the remains of seasonal structures, granaries, and farming infrastructure. The Havasupai began farming this and the other spring-fed and riparian areas of the canyon in at least the 12th century, and were still doing so when Europeans and Americans arrived in the 19th century.

In the late 1800s, canyon pioneer Ralph Cameron prospected in the area with little success, and in 1903 opened a tourist camp with tent cabins, gardens, orchards, cottonwood trees, a laundry, a kitchen, and even a telephone line to the South Rim. The National Park Service

Indian Garden

BEST PLACE TO WATCH THE SUNSET

The best place to watch the sunset from inside the Grand Canyon is from **Plateau Point,** at the end of an easy 1.5-mile (2.4-km) one-way trail from Indian Garden. The viewpoint sits high above the Colorado River and provides unfettered views up and down the inner gorge from its perch on the Tonto Platform. Unless you want to hike about 6 miles (9.7 km) back up to the South Rim with just your headlamp for comfort, the best way to see the sunset from Plateau Point is to camp at Indian Garden (permit and reservation required).

took control of the area in the early 1920s after the formation of Grand Canyon National Park in 1919. Today Indian Garden is a cool and green resting stop and campground along the Bright Angel Trail, a haven for tired up-hikers still facing the Bright Angel's steepest sections.

★ PLATEAU POINT

From Indian Garden, hike 1.5 miles (2.4 km) across the flat desert of the Tonto Platform to Plateau Point, an amazing cliff-edge viewpoint looking down on the roiling Colorado River snaking through the narrow inner gorge. The National Park Service discourages day hikes from the South Rim to Plateau Point in the summer (May-Sept.), but in spring or fall the strenuous 12-mile (19.3-km) round-trip hike is a wonderful day hike for experienced and fit hikers. The view and the atmosphere out here are best in the early to late evening, so if you want to take your time, obtain a permit and spend the night at Indian Garden's lush campground.

KAIBAB BRIDGE (BLACK BRIDGE)

There are very few ways to cross the Colorado River through Grand Canyon. Navajo Bridge, near Lees Ferry (River Mile 0), crosses over the river at Marble Canyon, about 90 miles (145 km) upriver from its confluence with Bright Angel Creek inside the inner gorge, where the second and third bridges span the roiling green flow.

The first one you come to, heading downriver and arriving at a crossroads of the main corridor trails near Phantom Ranch, is Kaibab Bridge, also known as Black Bridge, which is open to both hikers and mule trains. Can you imagine what it took to build this bridge, the main route across the river for all the mule trains that supply Phantom Ranch, in such a remote, inaccessible location? It was

Kaibab Bridge (Black Bridge)

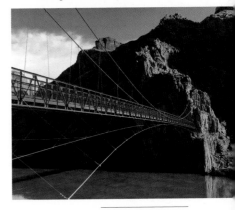

Plateau Point

1928, and maybe people were a bit tougher back then. It's the only way to explain it. Actually, it was a crew of mostly Havasupai men who did a lot of the heavy lifting, carrying the 550-foot-long (168-m) suspension cables down the trail in single file. However, as it always seems to be at Grand Canyon, it was the mules that did most of the work, carrying some 122 tons of materials from the rim.

The construction of Black Bridge really changed the way people visited the inner canyon. Before the early 1920s (when a temporary wooden suspension bridge went up prior to Black Bridge's completion), intrepid canyon explorers and suppliers had to slide across a cable over the Colorado in a metal cage about the size of one mule. This contraption had, since about 1907, been the only way to cross the river safely at Bright Angel Canyon; it was set up by early canyon pioneer and tourism entrepreneur David Rust, when what is now Phantom Ranch was a remote tent camp called Rust's Camp.

SILVER BRIDGE

Just downstream from Black Bridge and connecting the Bright Angel Trail with Phantom Ranch and the North Kaibab Trail, the Silver Bridge opened in 1960. The bridge holds up the trans-canyon water pipeline as it crosses the river on its way from Roaring Springs, below the North Rim, to all the faucets on the South Rim. It's open only to foot traffic.

Silver Bridge

BEST HIKES

The day hikes below all begin at or near Phantom Ranch, which is itself a 14-mile (22.5-km) trek from the North Rim.

CLEAR CREEK LOOP

DISTANCE: About 1.5 miles (2.4 km) round-trip
DURATION: 1-2 hours
ELEVATION GAIN: 826 feet (252 m)
EFFORT: Easy to moderate
TRAIL CONDITIONS: Dirt, rocky, narrow, dusty, steep, some sand
TRAILHEAD: About 0.3 mile (0.5 km) north of Phantom Ranch on North Kaibab Trail

A popular CCC-built trail near Phantom Ranch, the 1.5-mile (2.4-km) Clear Creek Loop takes you high above the river to **Phantom Overlook,** where there's an old stone bench and excellent views of the canyon and Phantom Ranch below. The rangers seem to recommend this hike the most, but, while it's not tough, it can be a little steep and rugged, especially if you're exhausted and sore. The views are, ultimately, well worth the pain.

PHANTOM RANCH TO RIBBON FALLS

DISTANCE: 11 miles (17.7 km) round-trip
DURATION: 5-6 hours to all day
ELEVATION GAIN: 1,174 feet (358 m)
EFFORT: Easy to moderate
TRAIL CONDITIONS: Dirt, rocky, some sand, narrow, high canyon walls
TRAILHEAD: North Kaibab Trail, on north side of Phantom Ranch

If you hiked in from the South Rim and you have a long, approximately 11-mile (17.7-km) round-trip day hike in you, head north on the **North Kaibab Trail** from Phantom Ranch to beautiful **Ribbon Falls,** a mossy, cool-water oasis just off the hot, dusty trail. The falls are indeed a ribbon of cold water falling hard off the rock cliffs, and you can scramble up the slickrock and through the green creek-side jungle and stand beneath the shower. Look

Clear Creek Loop (top); the Box, North Kaibab Trail (bottom)

TOP HIKE
RIVER TRAIL

DISTANCE: 1.5 miles (2.4 km) round-trip
DURATION: 1-2 hours
ELEVATION GAIN: Negligible
EFFORT: Easy
TRAIL CONDITIONS: Dirt, rocky, narrow, dusty
TRAILHEAD: Phantom Ranch, on north side of river; or at end of Bright Angel Trail on south side

This short hike is along the precipitous River Trail, high above the Colorado just south of Phantom Ranch. The Civilian Conservation Corps (CCC) blasted this skinny cliffside trail out of the rock walls in the 1930s to provide a link between the Bright Angel and the South Kaibab Trails. Heading out from Phantom, it's about a 1.5-mile (2.4-km) loop-plus-spur that takes you across both **suspension bridges** and high above the river. It's an easy walk with fantastic views and is a good way to get your sore legs stretched and moving again. And you are likely to see a bighorn sheep's cute little face poking out from the rocks and shadows on the steep cliffs.

for the sign for Ribbon Falls on the left side of the trail 5.5 miles (8.9 km) from Phantom. A section of this hike will also give you a chance to see the eerie, claustrophobic **"Box,"** one of the strangest and most exhilarating stretches of the North Kaibab (the last 4 mi/6.4 km of the trail going from north to south). This narrow stretch through the inner gorge is easy and flat but low and hot, boxed in by black Vishnu schist about 1.7 billion years old. Don't hike in the inner canyon after 10am in the summer.

COLORADO RIVER TRIPS

People who have been inside the Grand Canyon often have one of two reactions—either they can't wait to return, or they swear never to return. This is even the case for those intrepid souls who ride the great river, braving white-water roller coasters while looking forward to a star-filled evening—dry, and full of gourmet camp food—camping on a white beach deep in the gorge. To boat the Colorado is one of the most exciting and potentially life-changing trips the American West has to offer.

PLANNING

Rafting season in the canyon runs **April-October,** and there are myriad trips to choose from—from a 3-day long-weekend ride to an 18-day full-canyon epic. An **upper-canyon trip** will take you from River Mile 0 at Lees Ferry through the canyon to Phantom Ranch, while a **lower-canyon trip** begins at Phantom, requiring a hike down the Bright Angel with your gear on your back. Furthermore, you can choose between a motorized pontoon boat (as some three-quarters of rafters do), a paddleboat, a kayak, or some other combination. It all depends on what you want and what you can afford.

Expect to pay about $1,400 per person for a 3-day motor trip, $2,600 per person for a 6-day motor trip, $2,000 per person for a 6-day oar trip, and up to $5,000 per person for a 13-day oar trip. Many of the outfitters offer trips tailored to certain interests, such as trips with a naturalist or trips that make a lot of stops for hiking.

There are a few things you can do long before your trip that will serve you well on the river. The most important of these is to get in shape. Colorado River trips are incredibly active affairs. Not only will you probably have to hike into or out of the canyon via the punishing Bright Angel Trail, every day on the river there will be amazing, once-in-a-lifetime side trips on land—slick rocks over which to scramble, and steep trails (in the very loose sense of the word) to climb. Start training at least six months out with a steep trail or road and increase the difficulty over the months.

After you book your river trip, your guide company will send you a large packet of materials to look over. This generally includes information on what to expect from the trip, and offers suggestions about what to bring along and how to train for all the hiking. Make sure you read your packet over carefully and follow your guide's directions exactly.

Finally, it's a good idea to add travel insurance to the already steep price of your river trip. There's so

rafting on the Colorado River

much that could happen in the year or more between booking your trip and actually putting in at Lees Ferry or Phantom Ranch.

OUTFITTERS

Below is a list of the National Park Service-approved river trip outfitters. No other companies are allowed to guide trips through the canyon, so you must pick from among these highly respected and well-established companies.

- **Aramark-Wilderness River Adventures** (P.O. Box 171, Page, AZ; 928/645-3296 or 800/992-8022; www.riveradventures.com)

- **Arizona Raft Adventures** (4050 E. Huntington Dr., Flagstaff, AZ; 928/526-8246 or 800/786-7238; https://azraft.com)

- **Canyon Explorations/Expeditions** (675 W. Clay Ave., Flagstaff, AZ; 928/774-4559 or 800/654-0723; www.canyonexplorations.com)

- **Canyoneers** (7195 N. U.S. Hwy. 89, Flagstaff, AZ; 928/526-0924 or 800/525-0924; https://canyoneers.com)

- **Colorado River & Trail Expeditions** (P.O. Box 57575, Salt Lake City, UT; 801/261-1789 or 800/253-7328; www.crateinc.com)

- **Grand Canyon Dories** (P.O. Box 216, Altaville, CA; 209/736-0805 or 800/877-3679; www.oars.com)

- **Grand Canyon Expeditions** (P.O. Box 0, Kanab, UT; 435/644-2691 or 800/544-2691; www.gcex.com)

- **Grand Canyon Whitewater** (100 N. Humphreys St., Ste. 202, Flagstaff, AZ; 928/779-2979 or 800/343-3121; www.grandcanyonwhitewater.com)

- **Hatch River Expeditions** (5348 E. Burris Ln., Flagstaff, AZ; 928/526-4700 or 800/856-8966; www.hatchriverexpeditions.com)

- **O.A.R.S.** (P.O. Box 67, Angels Camp, CA; 209/736-2924 or 800/364-6277; www.oars.com)

- **Outdoors Unlimited** (6900 Townsend Winona Rd., Flagstaff, AZ; 800/637-7238; www.outdoorsunlimited.com)

- **Tour West** (P.O. Box 333, Orem, UT; 801/225-0755 or 800/453-9107; www.twriver.com)

- **Western River Expeditions** (7258 Racquet Club Dr., Salt Lake City, UT; 801/942-6669 or 800/453-7450; www.westernriver.com)

LEES FERRY TO PHANTOM RANCH

All river trips through the heart of Grand Canyon begin at Lees Ferry within the Glen Canyon National Recreation Area, which is River Mile 0 of the lower Colorado River. A popular trip is the 87 river miles (140 km) between Lees Ferry and Phantom Ranch in the inner gorge, often called the "upper-canyon trip." Such trips can last anywhere between 3-7 days, depending on if you're in a motorboat or running on oars, and can cost upward of $1,500 to more than $3,000 per person. River rafters encounter 19 major rapids on this trip, and it usually requires a hike out the Bright Angel Trail (about 4,500 ft/1,372 m up) to the South Rim. Your trip will begin the night before at a chain hotel in Flagstaff with a must-attend orientation meeting. Early the next morning you'll pile into a van with your new friends and head to Lees Ferry, about a two-hour drive. When you arrive at Lees Ferry, the bustling begins, packing everything onto the boat and getting everyone settled on board, and soon enough you'll be off on the green, cold-water river with the sandstone walls closing in.

The hike up the Bright Angel Trail to the South Rim from Phantom Ranch is 9.9 miles (15.9 km), and it's an arduous, long, and sometimes dispiriting trudge, but it doesn't have to be. You'll hike out with your guide, and there are plenty of places to rest. You can send your bag ahead of you on a mule by booking duffel service ahead of time (30 lbs/13.6 kg maximum, $76 one-way).

Navajo Bridge
MILE 4
You're just getting settled and used to being off dry land when, about 4 miles (6.4 km) on from Lees Ferry, you pass beneath Navajo Bridge, which crosses the river some 500 feet (152 m) above you. This is the last place for 342 miles (545 km) that you can drive across the Colorado River, the next spot being Hoover Dam near Las Vegas, Nevada. Give a wave to all those sad tourists up there looking down on you, wishing they were going downriver too. Keep an eye out for California condors as you pass through this well-known haunt.

Marble Canyon
MILE 5
About another mile (0.6 km) and you are officially in Grand Canyon. You'll know it when you see the ubiquitous top three layers appear here: the Kaibab Formation on top, the Toroweap Formation between,

and the Coconino sandstone below that. There's actually no marble in Marble Canyon; the name came from canyon explorer John Wesley Powell, who thought the polished walls resembled marble. Marble Canyon stretches all the way to the Colorado River's confluence with the Little Colorado River. While geologically Marble Canyon is part of Grand Canyon, it is still known by its historical name. It was added to Grand Canyon National Park in 1975.

boats at Lees Ferry (top); river trip passing below Navajo Bridge (bottom)

Soap Creek Rapid
MILE 11.2

It's not too long before you start to encounter the first rapids on the river, and you may already consider yourself a river-rat by the time you get through the **Badger Creek Rapid** at River Mile 7.8 and **Soap Creek Rapid** at Mile 11.2. There are nice sandy-beach campsites in this area, and it's where many first days on the river end. At Mile 12, there's a **carved inscription** on a rock commemorating the 1889 drowning death near here of Frank Brown, president of the Denver, Colorado, Canyon & Pacific Railroad Company, who along with engineer Robert B. Stanton journeyed into the canyon that year to complete a survey for a railroad project that, of course, never happened.

House Rock Rapid
MILE 17

At the mouth of the **Rider Canyon** tributary (down which rocks and other debris rush atop periodic flash floods, filling the river with rapid-creating materials), you encounter one

Vasey's Paradise

of the more difficult stretches of Marble Canyon—House Rock Rapid, where boats have been known to flip from time to time. A short scramble up Rider Canyon is a good way to stretch your legs and get off the boat for a while.

The Roaring Twenties
MILES 20-30

Almost universally described as akin to riding a roller coaster, the "Roaring Twenties" comprise **nine rapids** (including **Georgie, Hansbrough-Richards, Cave Springs,** and **Tiger Wash Rapids**), some spaced less than 1 mile (1.6 km) apart, making for a fast and super fun ride. You're soaked one minute, dry the next, then soaked again, and everybody's whooping and hollering all around you like kids at a waterpark. It's just pure fun, the river-running experience at its most enjoyable.

South Canyon
MILE 31

South Canyon, reached via an easy 0.3-mile (0.5-km) hike, is a popular spot to pull over and explore, especially in the beautiful area known as **Vasey's Paradise,** with cliffs covered in shaggy greenery and trickling white runnels falling close to the rocks. This area is also accessible from the North Rim and the House Rock Valley, so you may see hikers here as well as other river-runners. Nearby but not open to the public is **Stanton's Cave,** where archaeologists over the years have found the bones of extinct sloths and those mysterious bent-twig animal figures that were left by the canyon's ancient inhabitants. After the death of poor Frank Brown, Robert Stanton ended the 1889 railroad survey here, only to return the next year to continue the work down to the Gulf of California.

Redwall Cavern
MILES 33-50

Even if you can't afford to get there via the river, you've probably seen pictures of Redwall Cavern, which is one of the most popular and photographed places in the inner canyon. It's a huge chamber or amphitheater scooped out of the sandstone by eons of erosional forces. It's a must-stop along the river and truly amazing when seen up close. Cool and dark, Redwall Cavern is a wonderful place to hang out for a while during the infernal heat of a summertime river trip. There is no camping or fires allowed here. Moving on, the river bends around **Point Hansbrough,** a high, crumbling red-rock tower named for a member of the Brown-Stanton expedition, and through **President Harding Rapid** at Mile 43, a Class 4 rapid named for the 29th president.

Nankoweap Ruin Route
MILE 53

One of the highlights of an upper-canyon trip, this must-stop spot includes a steep but short (about 0.5 mi/0.8 km from the beach) hike to the **Nankoweap Granaries,** a small cliff ruin in which, around AD 1100, Ancestral Puebloans stored grain, seeds, and corn in dry, rodent-proof storehouses. The view of the river, atop which you've just traveled 53 miles (85 km), is amazing. There are several campsites in this area, and you may see some very tired hikers fresh off the 14-mile (22.5-km) **Nankoweap Trail** from the North Rim, one of Grand Canyon National Park's most difficult.

Little Colorado River Confluence
MILE 61

And so you have come to the confluence, where the **Little Colorado River**'s warmish, milky-blue water from limestone springs joins the cold,

Nankoweap Ruin

green waters of the Colorado. This spot, which marks the official end of Marble Canyon and start of **Granite Gorge** (also known as the **inner gorge**), is a sacred landscape for the Hopi, who believe the Sipapu, or navel, through which they entered this world is located here. The Hopi also gathered salt from large deposits nearby for centuries. Also here, under a sandstone cliff, is **Beamer's cabin,** a small stone structure built by pioneer and miner Ben Beamer in 1890 out of a Pueblo ruin. There is no camping or fishing allowed in this area. The warmer waters of the Little Colorado make it a favorite spot for the humpback chub and other endangered native fish.

Confluence to Inner Gorge
MILES 62–76

For the next 10 miles (16.1 km) or so you'll pass the Crash Canyon, near where a United DC-7 crashed in 1956, along with Temple Butte, Carbon Creek, Lava Canyon, Espejo Creek, Tanner Rapid, and Tanner Canyon. The river then widens at the **Unkar Rapid** and the **Unkar Delta** (taking their name from the Paiute word for "red stone"). The Unkar Delta, a big bend in the river around River Mile 72.5, was a home of farming Ancestral Puebloans between about AD 850–1200. Leaving the Unkar Delta, you'll pass Escalante Creek, Escalante Rapid, and Nevills Rapid, named for Norman D. Nevills, the first man to offer commercial river trips through the canyon (1938).

The Inner Gorge
MILE 76

The walls become narrow and close in a bit claustrophobically as you enter **Granite Gorge,** also known as the inner gorge. Suddenly you're surrounded by the oldest rocks on earth, the so-called basement rocks—dark-gray-and-black Vishnu schist and the red-and-pink intrusive igneous of the Zoroaster granite. The first really serious, major challenge comes at **Hance Rapid,** at River Mile 76.5, named for the famous canyon pioneer, guide, and raconteur John Hance. The rapid was created by flash floods from **Red Canyon,** through which the **New Hance Trail** leads toward the South

Inner Gorge (top and bottom)

Rim. As you approach the beach at the Bright Angel Creek confluence, near Phantom Ranch, you'll see the **Black and Silver Bridges** over the Colorado River, the only permanent foot crossings since Navajo Bridge far upriver.

Bright Angel Creek
MILE 88

Bright Angel Creek flows from Roaring Springs just below the North Rim, careening down **Bright Angel Canyon** along much of the **North Kaibab Trail,** spilling into the Colorado River just below Phantom Ranch and Bright Angel Campground, through which the creek flows below tall, shady cottonwood trees, singing sweetly to campers all day and night. Coined by who else but explorer John Wesley Powell, the name "Bright Angel" is repeated ad nauseum throughout the national park, and is said to have come about as a commentary on the creek's clarity in contrast to the then very muddy Colorado River and many of its flood-stage tributaries. Ancestral Puebloans once lived in this lush riparian area, and there's a small **ruin** reached by a trail above the river on the same bank as **Boat Beach,** which is bound to have a few relaxing hikers on it as you float in looking all tough and grizzled from your time upriver.

Phantom Ranch

One of the most peaceful and beautiful places on earth despite its hot desert setting, Phantom Ranch is a green paradise near the banks of Bright Angel Creek, shaded by tall cottonwoods and kept close by high, reddish canyon walls all around. This is considered the halfway point on the river, and it's the end of the upper portion and the start of the lower portion. If you're just doing the upper-canyon trip, this is where you'll hop off the water and start your grueling journey on land out to the South Rim. But before you head off, take a short walk up to the Phantom Ranch Canteen for a lemonade or a cold beer.

Bright Angel Creek

INNER CANYON FOOD OPTIONS

NAME	LOCATION	TYPE
Phantom Ranch Canteen	Phantom Ranch	shared tables

FOOD

In the entire inner canyon there is but one humble place to buy food, the Phantom Ranch Canteen, and most of their meals must be reserved about a year ahead of time. You can purchase a few snacks here without a reservation, but by and large you must pack all of your own food in and pack all of your trash out.

BEST PICNIC SPOTS

There are no picnic tables along the inner canyon trails, but it's important to stop, rest, and eat if you feel hungry; don't wait for the perfect picnic spot. Besides, no matter where you are along the Bright Angel, South Kaibab, or North Kaibab Trail when you feel those hunger pangs coming on, you are bound to find a spot and a view to go perfectly with your hiker's lunch.

Indian Garden

A cool strip of greenery in an otherwise sharp and hot desert, Indian Garden is a popular rest stop between the rim and river, a 9.6-mile (15.4-km) round-trip hike down the Bright Angel Trail from the South Rim. With picnic tables, shade trees, wildlife, and potable water, Indian Garden is an ideal spot for a deep-canyon picnic, whether you stop on your way into the canyon or on your way out.

Boat Beach
About 0.3 mile (0.5 km) from Phantom Ranch

Though there aren't any picnic tables on this small sunny beach on the Colorado River, there is soft sand and a mighty stream rolling by, sometimes carrying river-rafting trips through the Inner Gorge. Lay down a blanket and have a picnic lunch while you contemplate the river carving through the canyon. Don't forget to pack out all your trash.

CAMPING

Reservations

To stay overnight below the rim, you must obtain a **permit** from the **Backcountry Information Center** (928/638-7875; $10 plus $8 pp per night).

From March 1-November 14, you're allowed to spend up to two consecutive nights at a corridor campground (Bright Angel, Indian Garden, or Cottonwood). From

FOOD	PRICE	HOURS
breakfast, dinner, box lunch	moderate	reserve meals in advance

November 15-February 28, the limit is four consecutive nights.

Tips

The earliest you can apply for an inner canyon permit is 10 days before the first of the month that is four months before your proposed trip date. The easiest way to get a permit is to go to the **park's website** (www.nps.gov/grca), print out a backcountry permit request form, fill it out, and then fax it first thing in the morning on the date in question—for example, if you want to hike in October, you would **fax** (928/638-2125) your request May 20-June 1. On June 1 rangers will begin randomly processing all the requests for October, and they'll let you know in about three weeks. On the permit request form you'll indicate at which campgrounds you plan to stay. The permit is your reservation. For more information on obtaining a backcountry permit, call the **Backcountry Information Center** (928/638-7875; 8am-noon and 1pm-5pm daily year-round).

LODGING

STANDOUTS
★ Phantom Ranch
888/297-2757; www.grandcanyonlodges.com; dormitory $51 pp, 2-person cabin $149, $13 each additional person

Designed by Mary Jane Colter for the Fred Harvey Company in 1922, Phantom Ranch, the only noncamping accommodation inside the canyon, is a shady, peaceful place that you're likely to miss and yearn for once you've visited and left it behind. Perhaps Phantom's strong draw is less about its intrinsic pleasures and more about it being the only sign of civilization in a deep wilderness that can feel like the end of the world, especially after the 14-mile (22.5-km) hike in from the North Rim.

Phantom Ranch has 11 rustic, air-conditioned **cabins** and four hiker-only **dormitories.** The cabins vary in size, sleeping 2-10 people. Each cabin has a sink with cold water, a toilet, bedding, and towels. Hot-water sinks and showers are available in a separate "showerhouse" building, where towels, soap, and shampoo are also provided. There are two dormitories for men and two for women (families with children five or under must stay in a cabin). Each dormitory has five bunk beds, a toilet, and a shower. Bedding, towels, soap, and shampoo are provided. The dorms and the cabins are all heated in the winter and air-conditioned in the summer.

The lodge's center point is the

INNER CANYON CAMPGROUNDS

NAME	LOCATION	SEASON
Indian Garden	Bright Angel Trail (4.8 mi/7.7 km from South Rim)	year-round
Bright Angel	Near Phantom Ranch	year-round
Cottonwood Campground	North Kaibab Trail (6.8 mi/10.9 km from North Rim)	year-round (primitive mid-Oct.-mid-May)

INNER CANYON LODGING

NAME	LOCATION
★ Phantom Ranch	near the mouth of Bright Angel Canyon

Phantom Ranch Canteen, a welcoming, air-conditioned, beer- and lemonade-selling sight for anyone who has just descended one of the trails. There is no central lodge building at Phantom Ranch, but the canteen is the closest thing to it, with its family-style tables often filling up during the heat of the day with beer-drinkers and tale-tellers. The canteen offers two meals per day—**breakfast,** made up of eggs, pancakes, and thick slices of bacon ($23.65), and **dinner,** with a choice of steak ($47.91), stew ($29.43), or vegetarian ($29.43). The cantina

Bright Angel Campground (left); Phantom Ranch cabin (right)

SITES AND AMENITIES	RV LIMIT	PRICE	RESERVATIONS
15 tent sites; compost toilets; potable water	n/a	$8 for backcountry permit	first-come, first served
33 tent sites; flush toilets; potable water	n/a	$8 for backcountry permit	first-come, first served
11 tent sites; compost toilets; potable water mid-May– mid-Oct. only	n/a	$8 for backcountry permit	first-come, first served

SEASON	OPTIONS	PRICE
year-round	four hiker-only dorms, 11 cabins	dorm $51 per person; two-person cabin $149; lottery system reservations

also offers a **box lunch** ($20.85) with a bagel, fruit, and salty snacks. Reservations for meals are also difficult to come by. You must make them at least a year ahead.

Most nights and afternoons, a ranger based at Phantom Ranch will give a talk on some aspect of canyon lore, history, or science. These events are always interesting and well attended, even in the 110°F (43°C) heat of summer.

Phantom is located near the mouth of Bright Angel Canyon, within a few yards of clear, babbling Bright Angel Creek, and shaded by large cottonwoods, some of them planted in the 1930s by the Civilian Conservation Corps. There are several day hikes within easy reach, and the Colorado River and the two awesome suspension bridges that link one bank to the other are only about 0.4 mile (0.6 km) from the lodge.

A **lottery system** governs Phantom Ranch **reservations.** You have to enter the lottery between the 1st and 25th of the month 15 months prior to your proposed trip. You'll be notified at least 14 months before your trip if you won a stay. Go to www.grandcanyonlodges.com/lodging/phantom-ranch/lottery for more details.

INFORMATION AND SERVICES

Resthouses

There are several stone-and-wood resthouses along the corridor trails in which backpackers and day hikers can get out of the sun, have a rest, and, at some of them, even refill their water bottles.

On the **Bright Angel Trail,** look for **Mile-and-a-Half Resthouse** and **Three-Mile Resthouse,** 1.5 miles (2.4 km) and 3 miles (4.8 km), respectively, from the trailhead. Both resthouses have potable water available from mid-May to mid-October, emergency phones, and toilet facilities.

About 3 miles (4.8 km) down from Indian Garden, not long before you reach the river, the **River Resthouse** has an emergency phone and shade.

On the **South Kaibab Trail,** about 1.5 miles (2.4 km) from the trailhead, there are pit toilets at **Cedar Ridge,** but no resthouse or water.

Duffel Services

888/297-2757; www.grandcanyon-lodges.com; 30 lb (13.6 kg) maximum; $76 one-way

Xanterra, the park concessionaire that operates Phantom Ranch, offers a convenient and freeing mule-back duffel service between the South Rim and Phantom Ranch. The tough mule's burden becomes your salvation, as you breeze along the Bright Angel or the South Kaibab Trail with a light daypack on your back, free to look around and really take in the amazing landscape. It's easy to fit all you need for a few days in the canyon into a 30-pound (13.6-kg), 36 by 20 by 13-inch (91 by 51 by 33-cm) duffel bag. You provide the duffel bag and fill it yourself, then take it to the Xanterra Livery Barn (in Grand Canyon Village on the South Rim) to be weighed and accepted. You will need a reservation—make your duffel-service reservation at the same time you make all your other trip plans, up to a year out.

Inbound duffels headed to Phantom Ranch or nearby Boat Beach (this is a popular service with river-runners moving gear into and out of the canyon) must be at the Livery Barn by 3:30pm the day prior to the day they go down. Outbound duffels have to be at the Phantom Ranch loading area near the canteen no later than 6:30am on the day they are going out. You can pick up your duffels between

3pm–4pm at the Livery Barn on the day that they come out, or between 6:30am–4pm the next day.

Emergencies

There are a lot of things that can go wrong on a backpacking trip into Grand Canyon. Most of these are completely avoidable if you plan ahead, have respect for the difficulty of what you are doing, follow the rules, and pay attention.

If you or one of your party is injured or becomes sick while hiking on the corridor trails, head to one of the **emergency phones** at the resthouses, developed campgrounds, and ranger stations (Indian Garden and Phantom Ranch), and at the junction of the South Kaibab and Tonto Trails. Ask passersby to help get the message to rangers on the rim. Don't leave the injured or sick person alone. Soon enough, there will probably be a helicopter hovering over, ready to evacuate the patient to the rim and safety. While you may be able to get cell service in a few places inside the canyon if you're lucky, it should in no way be relied on for getting help.

There are regular ranger patrols below the rim on the Bright Angel, South Kaibab, and North Kaibab Trails, and at the ranger stations at Indian Garden on the Bright Angel Trail and Phantom Ranch in the inner gorge. River guides are generally trained for emergencies and first aid, and they will typically know a way to quickly contact civilization from the river.

TRANSPORTATION
Getting There
South Kaibab Trailhead

On the **South Rim,** you have to take the **free shuttle** to the South Kaibab Trailhead or else have somebody drop you off. There are no cars allowed near the trailhead and no overnight parking allowed. Take the **Kaibab/Rim Route (Orange)** to access the trailhead.

North Kaibab Trailhead

On the **North Rim,** to get from the **Grand Canyon Lodge**—the park's only accommodations on the North Rim—to the North Kaibab Trailhead, take the **hiker shuttle** (daily May 15-Oct. 15; $7 for first person, $4 for each additional person), which leaves the lodge twice daily first thing in the morning. Tickets must be purchased the day before at the lodge.

Grand Canyon West

WEST RIM

Much of the hard, remote, and bewitching land around Grand Canyon National Park belongs to Native American tribes to whom the great gorge is an eternal and sacred place. This is a world of vast high-desert plains and evergreen plateaus, of wind-sculpted buttes and narrow slickrock canyons, of lonely bunchgrass sweeps and red dirt.

Alternative rims and routes into Grand Canyon await tourists and explorers to the west of the South Rim, where the Hualapai (WALL-uh-pie) Tribe watches over the Grand Canyon Skywalk, a glass horseshoe hovering over the gorge. Since the Skywalk opened in 2007, the remote Grand Canyon West has become a fairly busy tourist attraction up on the West Rim.

The Skywalk is about a two-hour drive from the Hualapai Reservation's capital, Peach Springs, which is located along Route 66 west of Seligman. Although there's not much in Peach Springs other than a lodge and a few scattered houses, it makes an obvious base for a visit to Grand Canyon West. The tribe's Hualapai River Runners offer a one-day rafting trip on the river.

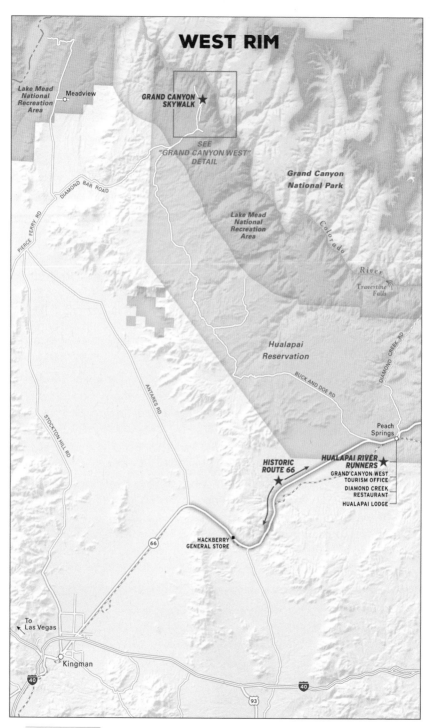

WEST RIM

GRAND CANYON SKYWALK ★

Lake Mead National Recreation Area

Meadview

SEE "GRAND CANYON WEST" DETAIL

Grand Canyon National Park

DIAMOND BAR ROAD

PIERCE FERRY RD

Lake Mead National Recreation Area

Colorado

River

Travertine Falls

Hualapai Reservation

STOCKTON HILL RD

ANTARES RD

BUCK AND DOE RD

DIAMOND CREEK RD

Peach Springs

HISTORIC ROUTE 66 ★

HUALAPAI RIVER RUNNERS ★
GRAND CANYON WEST TOURISM OFFICE
DIAMOND CREEK RESTAURANT
HUALAPAI LODGE

66

HACKBERRY GENERAL STORE

To Las Vegas

Kingman

40

40

93

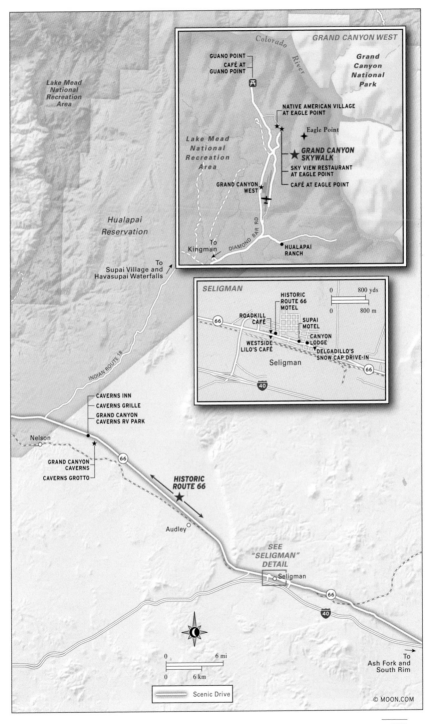

GRAND CANYON WEST

Colorado River

Grand Canyon National Park

GUANO POINT
CAFÉ AT GUANO POINT

Lake Mead National Recreation Area

NATIVE AMERICAN VILLAGE AT EAGLE POINT

Eagle Point

GRAND CANYON SKYWALK

SKY VIEW RESTAURANT AT EAGLE POINT

CAFÉ AT EAGLE POINT

GRAND CANYON WEST

To Kingman

DIAMOND BAR RD

HUALAPAI RANCH

Lake Mead National Recreation Area

Hualapai Reservation

To Supai Village and Havasupai Waterfalls

INDIAN ROUTE 18

SELIGMAN

0   800 yds
0   800 m

66

ROADKILL CAFÉ

HISTORIC ROUTE 66 MOTEL

SUPAI MOTEL

CANYON LODGE

WESTSIDE LILO'S CAFÉ

DELGADILLO'S SNOW CAP DRIVE-IN

Seligman

40

66

CAVERNS INN
CAVERNS GRILLE
GRAND CANYON CAVERNS RV PARK

Nelson

66

GRAND CANYON CAVERNS
CAVERNS GROTTO

HISTORIC ROUTE 66

Audley

SEE "SELIGMAN" DETAIL

Seligman

66

40

To Ash Fork and South Rim

0   3   6 mi
0   6 km

Scenic Drive

© MOON.COM

TOP 3

1. GRAND CANYON SKYWALK: Stand on a transparent glass platform and look straight down at the canyon floor 4,000 feet (1,219 m) below (page 166).

2. HISTORIC ROUTE 66: Drive the longest remaining stretch of the Mother Road, exploring the charming holdouts of American road-culture (page 169).

3. HUALAPAI RIVER RUNNERS: Ride the Colorado River the easy way on the only one-day rafting trip in the canyon (page 172).

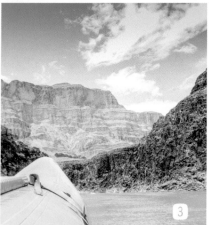

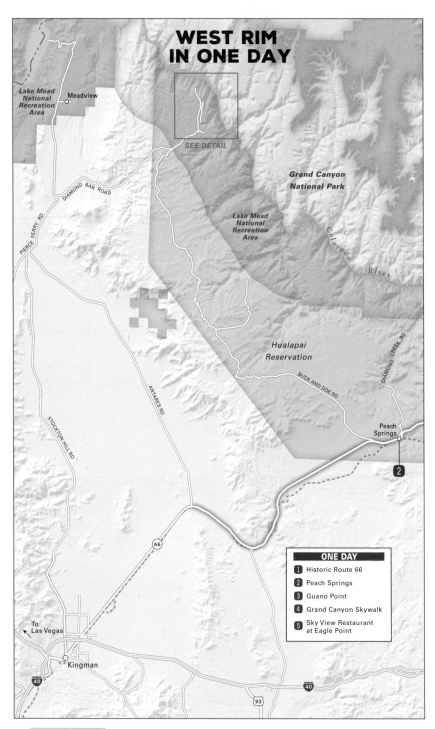

WEST RIM IN ONE DAY

SEE DETAIL

Lake Mead National Recreation Area

Meadview

Grand Canyon National Park

Lake Mead National Recreation Area

Colorado River

DIAMOND BAR ROAD

PIERCE FERRY RD

Hualapai Reservation

BUCK AND DOE RD

DIAMOND CREEK RD

Peach Springs

ANTARES RD

STOCKTON HILL RD

2

66

ONE DAY
1. Historic Route 66
2. Peach Springs
3. Guano Point
4. Grand Canyon Skywalk
5. Sky View Restaurant at Eagle Point

To Las Vegas

Kingman

I-40

93

I-40

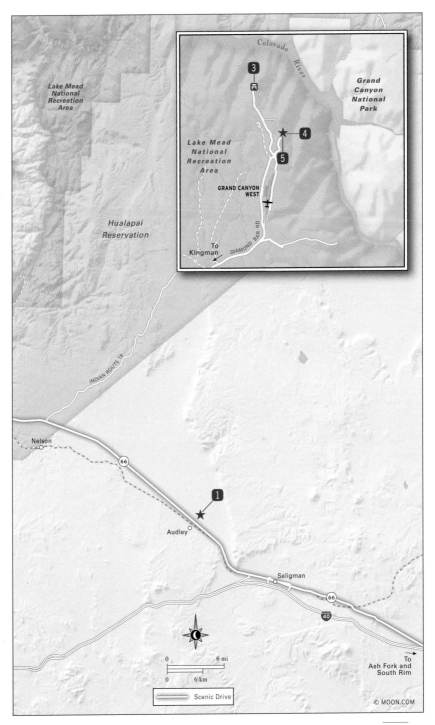

Lake Mead National Recreation Area

Grand Canyon National Park

3

Colorado River

Lake Mead National Recreation Area

★ **4**

5

GRAND CANYON WEST

To Kingman

DIAMOND BAR RD

Hualapai Reservation

INDIAN ROUTE 18

Nelson

66

1 ★

Audley

Seligman

66

40

To Ash Fork and South Rim

0   6 mi

0   6 km

Scenic Drive

© MOON.COM

3

WEST RIM IN ONE DAY

1 From Grand Canyon's South Rim, exit Interstate 40 at Ashfork and drive **Historic Route 66** to Peach Springs (62 mi/99.8 km), the capital of the Hualapai Nation.

2 Once arrived in **Peach Springs,** stop at the Hualapai Lodge for the latest information on visiting Grand Canyon West, and eat at Diamond Creek restaurant.

3 From Peach Springs, drive approximately 2 hours to Grand Canyon West ($45 pp general admission). You must park your car and use the free hop-on, hop-off shuttle to get around. Take the shuttle first to **Guano Point** for a gorgeous view of the Grand Canyon and the Colorado River. Hike the 0.8-mile (1.3-km) round-trip Highpoint Trail and explore the remains of the old aerial tramway built in the 1950s to serve a guano mine.

4 Next, take the shuttle to Eagle Point and the **Grand Canyon Skywalk.** If you dare, buy a ticket ($23 pp on top of general admission) and shuffle onto the glass horseshoe hovering 4,000 feet above the canyon floor.

5 Grand Canyon West does not allow outside food. If you get hungry, eat at the **Sky View Restaurant at Eagle Point,** which has amazing views of the canyon and the Skywalk.

Avoid the Crowds

Grand Canyon West is tour-bus country, with most tours originating in Las Vegas, and it's really not possible to avoid crowds at the Skywalk. Going early and **taking your own vehicle** as opposed to booking a tour is the best strategy. Also consider skipping the Skywalk and heading straight for **Guano Point,** an equally beautiful but less crowded West Rim viewpoint.

HIGHLIGHTS

Grand Canyon West (5001 Diamond Bar Rd.; 928/769-2636 or 888/868-9378; www.grandcanyonwest.com; 9am-sundown daily; $39 general admission, $20 add-on for Skywalk, $19 add-on for meal) is the Hualapai Reservation's tourist area, comprising several viewpoints on the western rim of Grand Canyon and the Skywalk.

A general admission ticket gets you on the free hop-on, hop-off shuttle to Eagle Point, where the **Skywalk** is located, and **Guano Point.** (Getting around by private vehicle is not permitted at Grand Canyon West; there is a large parking area where you can leave your car and pick up the shuttle.) It's a good idea to book your general admission tickets and add-ons before you travel out to this remote sight.

Guano Point

★ GRAND CANYON SKYWALK

$59 for general admission with Skywalk ticket

The Skywalk is as much an art installation as it is a tourist attraction. A horseshoe-shaped glass and steel platform jutting out 70 feet (21 m) from the canyon rim, it appears futuristic surrounded by the rugged, remote western canyon. Although the long drive and the price can be deterrents to visiting the Skywalk, there is something of the thrill ride to the experience. Some people

VISITING NATIVE AMERICAN RESERVATIONS

While the Native American communities in the canyonlands vary greatly in their cultures, histories, and ambitions for tourism, there are a few general rules to keep in mind when visiting their lands.

First and foremost, never forget that reservations are not national parks. Treat Native American reservations as you would private property. That means asking permission before entering them, and abiding by any permit rules each nation may have. Don't take pictures without asking first, and don't drive off road for any reason—that's somebody's land and livelihood. If you are lucky enough to be invited to watch a dance or other ceremony, treat it as you would any religious observance—with quiet reverence.

Again, remember that not all Native American nations are the same; research the requirements and the rules of each individual reservation before visiting.

can't handle it: They walk out a few steps, look down through the glass at the canyon 4,000 feet (1,219 m) below, and head for (seemingly) more solid ground. It's all perfectly safe, but it doesn't feel that way if you are subject to vertigo. Another drawback of this site is that you are not allowed to take your camera out on the Skywalk. If you want a record of this adventure, you have to buy a "professional" photo taken by somebody else. You have to store all of your possessions, including your camera, in a locker before stepping out on the glass, with covers on your shoes.

NATIVE AMERICAN VILLAGE AT EAGLE POINT

Admission included with general admission ticket

While the Skywalk is the star of Eagle Point, don't miss the illuminating experience of a self-guided stroll across the windswept, sun-beaten rim through a re-created Native American Village. The walk is easy and mostly flat, but there is little shade so make sure to bring a hat and water. The trail passes examples of traditional dwellings and other structures associated with several of the tribes closely tied to the Grand Canyon, including the homes and sweat lodges of the Hualapai and Havasupai tribes of

Native American Village at Eagle Point

BEST PLACE TO WATCH THE SUNSET

The best place to watch the sunset at Grand Canyon West is from **Guano Point.** Here you'll find expansive views of the western Grand Canyon and the Colorado River, allowing for long looks at the evening redness in the west. (Just don't forget: If you stay to watch the sunset here you'll have to drive back to civilization in the dark.)

the western canyon, as well as those of the Navajo and Hopi. The tepee associated with Great Plains tribes is also on display, and there's a profusion of information about Indigenous lifeways featured along the way. In the center of the village there's an amphitheater with daily performances and presentations of Native American arts and culture.

GUANO POINT

This scenic point has wonderful views of the western Grand Canyon and the Colorado River, as well as rimside café with outdoor seating. Take a hike here along the 0.8-mile (1.3-km) round-trip **Highpoint Trail** and explore the remains of the old aerial tramway built in the 1950s to serve a guano mine.

Guano Point

SCENIC DRIVES

★ HISTORIC ROUTE 66

DRIVING DISTANCE: 84 miles (135.2 km) from Ash Fork to Indian Route 18; 62.2 miles (100.1 km) from Ash Fork to Peace Springs

DRIVING TIME: 2 hours (from Ash Fork to Indian Route 18 and the turn-off to the trailhead to Havasupai); 1 hour (from Ash Fork to Peach Springs and the turn-off to Grand Canyon West)

START: Ash Fork

END: Indian Route 18 (for Havasupai) or Antares Road turnoff (for Grand Canyon West)

The longest remaining stretch of Historic Route 66 runs from Ash Fork, on I-40, through the dry grasslands, cholla forests, and jagged hills of northwestern Arizona west to Topock, a tiny town on the Colorado River. You can drive a good portion of this stretch of Route 66 on your way to Grand Canyon West from the South Rim. Along the way, you'll see wind-swept landscapes, rocky hills, and a few quirky sights that old-school road-trippers will love. To get to the starting point from the South Rim, take AZ 64 south to I-40, and then head west to the Ash Fork exit, an 80-mile (129-km), 1.5-hour drive.

The tiny roadside settlement of **Seligman,** 26.5 miles (43 km) west of Ash Fork, holds on tight to its Route 66 heritage. Fewer than 500 full-time residents live in this old ranching hub, railroad center, and Route 66 stop, but there is often, especially on summer weekends, twice that number in tourists driving through and stopping for a bite to eat and a look around the gift shops. Tour buses and large gangs of motorcycling Europeans even stop here and crowd the one-strip town on occasion. John Lasseter, codirector of the 2006 Disney-Pixar film *Cars,* has said that he based the movie's fictional town of Radiator Springs partly on Seligman, which, like Radiator Springs, nearly died out when it was bypassed by I-40 in the late 1970s.

In Seligman, **Delgadillo's Snow Cap Drive-In** (301 E. Chino Ave., Seligman; 928/422-3291; 10am-6pm daily; $5-10) is a famous food shack

Old Route 66 (left); Seligman (right)

whose family of owners have been dedicated to feeding, entertaining, and teasing Route 66 travelers for generations. They serve a mean chili burger, a famous "cheeseburger with cheese," and much more, but the food's not really the point. Originally built in 1953 out of found lumber, the Snow Cap has become one of the stars of the back-to-Route-66 movement. There's a lot to look at outside: a 1936 Chevy and other old cars (all of them with big eyes on their windshields, à la the film *Cars*), railroad junk, and several very silly signs; and inside, the close walls are covered with the business cards of customers from all over the world. There will likely be a stand-up wait, especially on summer weekends, and you *will* be teased, especially if you have a question that requires a serious answer.

About 24.6 miles (40 km) west of Seligman, **Grand Canyon Caverns** (Route 66, mile marker 115; 928/422-3223; www.gccaverns.com; 8am-6pm daily summer, 10am-4pm daily winter; $21-29 adults, $10.95-17.95 children 6-12) is an old-school Route 66 tourist trap (in the best sense of the phrase) with guided underground tours of North America's largest dry cave. The main tour lasts about 45 minutes and takes you about 0.8 mile (1.2 km) through the limestone cavern, where crystals and other strange rock formations hide in the darkness, but not before you descend 21 stories (210 feet/64 m) beneath the earth in an elevator. They also offer a shorter tour that is wheelchair accessible.

From Seligman, it's about a 30-mile (48-km) drive to **Indian Route 18,** which is the turnoff for Havasupai. If you're headed to Grand Canyon West, it's a 37-mile (60-km) drive from Seligman to **Peach Springs,** where Hualapai Lodge is located. From Peach Springs, it's another 29 miles (47 km) west along Route 66 to the **Antares Road** turnoff that heads toward Grand Canyon West.

Between Peach Springs and Antares Road, you'll find it hard to resist making one more classic Route 66 stop: the picture-ready **Hackberry General Store** (11255 E. Hwy. 66, Hackberry; 928/769-2605; www.

Delgadillo's Snow Cap Drive-In (top);
Hackberry General Store (bottom)

hackberrygeneralstore.com; 9am–6pm daily) and junkyard museum. With a cherry-red, 1957 Corvette parked conspicuously out front, the general store offers cold sodas, snacks, souvenirs, and a lot to look at, including some really cool road-map murals on the walls by artist Bob Waldmire.

DIAMOND CREEK ROAD

DRIVING DISTANCE: 19 miles (31 km)
DRIVING TIME: 45 minutes
START: Peach Springs
END: Colorado River

You can drive close to the Colorado River's edge yourself along the 19-mile (31-km) Diamond Creek Road through a dry, scrubby landscape scattered with cacti. The road provides the only easy access to the river's edge between Lees Ferry, not far from the North Rim, and Pearce Ferry, near Lake Mead. You need a permit to drive the road; obtain one at the Hualapai Lodge in Peach Springs (the road is just across Route 66 from the lodge). A tribal police officer may check it at some point along the road.

Start at the Hualapai Lodge and drive 0.5 mile (0.8 km) to Diamond Creek Road. At the end of the road, where Diamond Creek marries the Colorado, there's a sandy beach by an enchanting, lush oasis, and, of course, there's that big river rolling by.

The route is best negotiated in a high-clearance SUV; you have to cross Diamond Creek six times as the dirt road winds down through Peach Springs Canyon, dropping some 3,400 feet (1,036 m) from its beginning at Peach Springs on Route 66. The creek is susceptible to flash floods during the summer and winter rainy seasons, so call ahead to check road conditions (928/769-2230).

Diamond Creek Road

RIVER RAFTING

★ HUALAPAI RIVER RUNNERS

Grand Canyon West; 928/769-2636 or 888/868-9378; www.grandcanyonwest.com; May-Oct.; $450 pp

Due to the hefty advance planning, time commitment, and rugged conditions, a Colorado River adventure in other parts of the Grand Canyon isn't something that the average tourist is likely to try, but in Grand Canyon West, the experience is much more accessible. Hualapai River Runners offer the Grand Canyon's only one-day river rafting experience, and it's worth the steep price tag. Hualapai river guides will pick you up in a van early in the morning at the Hualapai Lodge in Peach Springs and drive you to the Colorado via the rough Diamond Creek Road, where you'll float downstream in a motorboat over roiling white-water rapids and smooth and tranquil stretches. You'll stop for lunch on a beach and take a short hike through a watery side canyon to beautiful **Travertine Falls.** At the end of the trip, a helicopter picks you out of the canyon and drops you on the rim near the Skywalk. It's expensive, yes, but if you want to ride the river without a lot of preplanning and camping, this is the way to do it. Along the way the Hualapai guides tell stories about this end of the Grand Canyon, sprinkled with tribal history and lore.

Hualapai River Runners offers one-day rafting trips.

Colorado River

WEST RIM FOOD OPTIONS

NAME	LOCATION	TYPE
Sky View Restaurant	Eagle Point/Grand Canyon Skywalk	sit-down
Café at Guano Point	Guano Point	outdoor quick service
★ Diamond Creek	Peach Springs	sit-down restaurant
Caverns Grille	Grand Canyon Caverns, Historic Route 66, mile marker 115	sit-down restaurant
Caverns Grotto	Grand Canyon Caverns, Historic Route 66, mile marker 115	sit-down restaurant
Roadkill Café	502 W. Route 66, Seligman	sit-down restaurant
Westside Lilo's Café	22855 W. Old Hwy. 66, Seligman	diner

FOOD

The dining scene at Grand Canyon West is not great. There are two eateries (a restaurant at Eagle Point and a café at Guano Point) with great views of the canyon, but limited food options. As an alternative, consider eating at the excellent restaurant at the Hualapai Lodge in Peach Springs.

Along Route 66, there are eateries at Grand Canyon Caverns and Seligman. Bringing outside food and beverages to Grand Canyon West is not permitted.

STANDOUTS
Diamond Creek
900 Route 66; 928/769-2230 or 928/769-2636; www.grandcanyon-west.com; 6am-9pm daily; $10-15
The Hualapai Lodge's restaurant, Diamond Creek, serves American and Native American dishes. The Hualapai taco (similar to the Navajo taco, with beans and meat piled high on a fluffy slab of fry bread) and the Hualapai stew (with luscious sirloin tips and vegetables swimming in a delicious, hearty

FOOD	PRICE	HOURS
burgers and sandwiches	$19 add-on to Grand Canyon West admission ticket	9am-5pm daily
American comfort food; typically three options: beef, chicken, vegetarian	budget	8am-6pm daily
American and Native American food	budget	6am-9pm daily
American food	budget	noon-8pm daily
American food	splurge (includes Grand Canyon Caverns tour)	noon-4:45pm and 5pm-9pm daily
Western food	budget	7am-9pm daily
American food	budget	6am-9pm daily

broth) are both recommended. The restaurant also offers a heaping plate of delicious spaghetti—great if you're carbo-loading for a big hike to Havasupai—and a few vegetarian choices, good chili, and pizza.

Roadkill Café (left); Grand Canyon Caverns (right)

WEST RIM CAMPGROUNDS

NAME	LOCATION	SEASON
Grand Canyon Caverns RV Park	Grand Canyon Caverns, Historic Route 66, mile marker 115	year-round

WEST RIM LODGING

NAME	LOCATION
Hualapai Ranch	Grand Canyon West
Hualapai Lodge	Peach Springs
Caverns Inn	Grand Canyon Caverns, Historic Route 66, mile marker 115
Supai Motel	134 W. Chino St., Seligman
Historic Route 66 Motel	22750 W. Route 66, Seligman
Canyon Lodge	114 E. Chino St., Seligman

CAMPING

While there are rustic cabins for rent at Grand Canyon West, the best RV Park and camping in the region are at Grand Canyon Caverns along Old Route 66 near Peach Springs. They offer 48 sites with full hookups for RVs of all sizes as well as hotel rooms and tent sites.

Tips

This is a popular area for RVers, so make sure to reserve your spot ahead of time.

LODGING

Reservations and Tips

In Grand Canyon West, the only accommodation is **Hualapai Ranch**, where you can take a zipline ride or go horseback riding, in addition to staying overnight. There are several small, locally owned motels in Seligman.

SITES AND AMENITIES	RV LIMIT	PRICE	RESERVATIONS
48 RV sites; tent sites; flush toilets; showers; potable water; full hookups	none	$40-50	www.gccaverns.com

SEASON	OPTIONS	PRICE
year-round	cabins	cabins starting at $125
year-round	hotel rooms	rooms starting at $150
year-round	motel rooms	rooms starting at $117
year-round	motel rooms	rooms starting at $69
year-round	motel rooms	rooms starting at $69
year-round	hotel rooms	rooms starting at $70

Hualapai Ranch

Historic Route 66 Motel

INFORMATION AND SERVICES

All of the services in the Grand Canyon West area are located in Peach Springs, which is the Hualapai Reservation's capital.

Visitor Centers

Grand Canyon West Tourism Office

Hualapai Lodge, 900 AZ 66, Peach Springs; 928/769-2230; https://grandcanyonwest.com

The Grand Canyon West tourism office is in Hualapai Lodge in Peach Springs along Historic Route 66, about two hours from the Sky Walk. The one-day river trips start from the lodge. Stop here and make sure you have directions and supplies before heading out on the long drive to Grand Canyon West. There's also a small store and a good restaurant attached to the lodge.

TRANSPORTATION

Getting There

Most people visit the Hualapai Reservation's Grand Canyon West and The Skywalk from Las Vegas. It's a long drive from the South Rim—you'd need at least two extra days.

From the South Rim

The best way to get to Grand Canyon West from the South Rim includes a jaunt on the longest remaining portion of Route 66 (page 169). From the South Rim, take **AZ 64** south to **I-40,** and then head west to the Ash Fork exit. Drive west on Route 66, passing Seligman and Peach Springs, which are good stops for services and Route 66 nostalgia. Twenty-nine miles (47 km) west of Peach Springs, turn right on Antares Road, leaving Route 66. Drive 32 miles (52 km) on Antares Road, then turn right onto Pearce Ferry Road. Drive 3 miles (4.8 km), and then turn right on Diamond Bar Road to drive 21 miles (34 km) to the only entrance to Grand Canyon West. The drive from Peach Springs to Grand Canyon West is 85 miles (137 km) and takes about 2 hours. The total drive from the South Rim to Grand Canyon West is about 225 miles (360 km) and takes about 4.5 hours.

From Las Vegas

Hualapai Reservation's Skywalk is only 125 miles (201 km) from Las Vegas, so it makes sense to include this as a side trip if you're headed to the South Rim from Vegas. Take U.S. 93 out of Las Vegas, heading south for about 65 miles (105 km) to mile marker 42, where you'll see the Dolan Springs/Meadview City/Pearce Ferry exit. Turn north onto Pearce Ferry Road. About 30 miles (48 km) in, turn east on Diamond Bar Road. Then it's about 20 miles (32 km) to Grand Canyon West. The entire drive takes about 2.5 hours

Parking and Shuttles

Once you arrive at Grand Canyon West, you must park your vehicle and ride the free hop-on, hop-off shuttle between the viewpoints. There is a large parking area where you can leave your car and pick up the shuttle.

Gas

Gas is only available in an emergency at Grand Canyon West. Ask at the gift shop if you run out. You must gas up at Peach Springs or elsewhere along Old Route 66 from I-40 or Hwy. 93 from Las Vegas.

Havasu Falls

HAVASU CANYON

Deep within the western canyon, members of the Havasupai Tribe (Havasu 'Baaja, the "people of the blue-green water") live in a small village above a series of beautiful blue-green waterfalls. Thousands of tourists from all over the world flock to Havasupai land every year just to see the falls, to swim in their pools, and to visit one of the most remote hometowns in North America.

The Havasupai (Pai means "people" in the Yuman language) have been living in Grand Canyon since at least the 12th century, tending small irrigated fields of corn, melons, beans, and squash, and small orchards of peach, apple, and apricot trees. For centuries the Havasupai farmed in Havasu Canyon and in other spring-fed areas of Grand Canyon—Indian Garden along the Bright Angel Trail and Santa Maria Spring along the Hermit Trail—in the summer and then hunted and gathered on the rim during the winter, ancient patterns that were disrupted by the settling of northern Arizona in the late 19th century. Today the Havasupai rely primarily on tourism to their little hidden oasis in Grand Canyon.

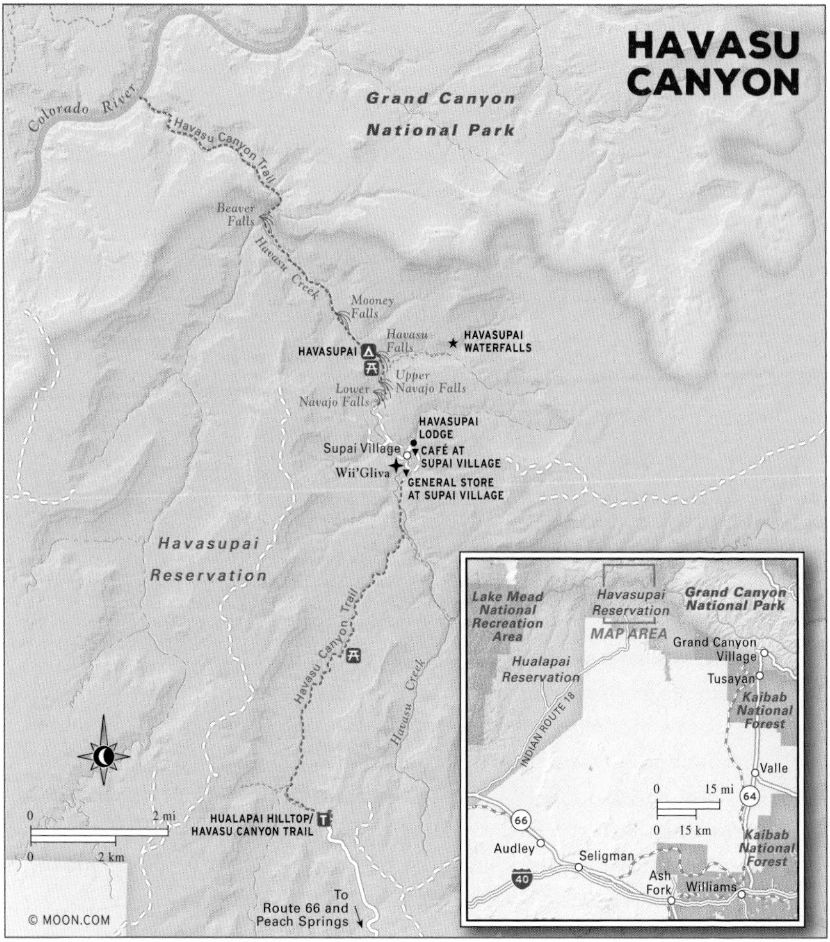
HAVASU CANYON
Grand Canyon National Park
Colorado River
Havasu Canyon Trail
Beaver Falls
Havasu Creek
Mooney Falls
Havasu Falls
HAVASUPAI
HAVASUPAI WATERFALLS
Upper Navajo Falls
Lower Navajo Falls
HAVASUPAI LODGE
Supai Village
CAFÉ AT SUPAI VILLAGE
Wii'Gliva
GENERAL STORE AT SUPAI VILLAGE
Havasupai Reservation
Havasu Canyon Trail
Havasu Creek
0 2 mi
0 2 km
HUALAPAI HILLTOP/ HAVASU CANYON TRAIL
To Route 66 and Peach Springs
© MOON.COM
Lake Mead National Recreation Area
Havasupai Reservation
MAP AREA
Grand Canyon National Park
Grand Canyon Village
Tusayan
Hualapai Reservation
INDIAN ROUTE 18
Kaibab National Forest
Valle
0 15 mi
0 15 km
64
66
Audley
Seligman
40
Ash Fork
Williams
Kaibab National Forest

HIGHLIGHTS

HAVASUPAI WATERFALLS

928/448-2121; http://theofficial-havasupaitribe.com; entry fee $50 plus $10 environmental fee

Located on the land of the Havasupai, these striking waterfalls draw travelers from all over the world. Heavy with lime, the waters of Havasu Creek flow an almost tropical blue green. The creek passes below the weathered red walls of the western Grand Canyon and cuts Havasu Canyon. Along the way, it drops over ledges and fills hollows in the rocks, creating blue-green waterfalls and pools that enchant with their beauty.

A visit to Havasupai and the waterfalls takes some planning. The waterfalls are not accessible by car, and the tribe requires that you

BEST PLACE TO WATCH THE SUNSET

The best place to watch the sunset in Havasupai is from the banks of **Havasu Falls** or one of the other waterfalls nearby. The fading light of the sun dancing on the blue-green waters makes for a show you won't soon forget. Sit back, relax, listen to the soothing sounds of water falling, and watch the sky light up and then slowly fade to one of the darkest nights you'll ever see.

stay overnight and have a reservation to visit the falls; no day trips are allowed. To make a reservation for the **Havasu Canyon campground,** you have to reserve a space online at www.havasupaireservations.com beginning at 8am on February 1 of the year you want to go. Camping permits sell out fast! To make reservations for the **Havasupai Lodge** (which you should do far in advance), located in Supai Village, call 928/448-2111 or visit www.havasupaireservations.com.

It's a long hike (10 mil/16.1 km) to get to Havasu Falls. If you don't want to hike in, you can arrange to **rent a mule** (928/448-2121, 928/448-2174, or 928/448-2180; www.officialhavasupaitribe.com; $400 round-trip to campground) or hire a helicopter from **Airwest** (623/516-2790; 10am-1pm Sun.-Mon. and Thurs.-Fri. Mar. 15-Oct. 15, 10am-1pm Sun. and Fri. Oct. 16-Mar. 14; $85 one-way). The best months to visit are September-October and April-June; it's unbearably hot in the deep summer, when you can't hike except in the very early morning.

The falls are listed below in the order you'll encounter them on your hike. Havasu and Mooney are the big standouts.

Havasu Falls

Upper Navajo Falls and Lower Navajo Falls

Underwhelming by Havasu Falls standards, **Upper Navajo Falls** (1.3 mi/2.1 km from the village) gained steam after a flash flood in 2008 rearranged the falls closest to the village. These falls are also referred to as Fifty Foot Falls because they fall about 50 feet (15 m) in a light-blue and foaming white rush. Just downstream is **Lower Navajo Falls,** also called Little Navajo Falls cascade, where water falls in multiple streams from about 30 feet (9 km) into an inviting swimming pool.

Havasu Falls

Perhaps the most famous of the canyon's blue-green falls, Havasu Falls appears all of a sudden as you get closer to the campground on the hike in. About 1.5 miles (2.5 km) from the village, Havasu Falls drops some 100 feet (30 m) into magical blue, calcium-carbonate-green, foamy white and Arizona-sky turquoise pools hemmed in by natural travertine dams. You can even swim behind the falls and watch the world through a veil of falling water. Few hikers refuse to toss their packs aside and strip to their swimsuits when they see Havasu Falls for the first time.

Mooney Falls

The other major waterfall, Mooney Falls, is another mile (1.6 km) down the trail from Havasu Falls, through the campground (2.3 mi/3.7 km from the village). This is the highest waterfall in the canyon, dropping some 190 feet (58 m) in a narrow foamy-white stream into large swimming pool, which is a bit colder than the others because of shady location. It's not easy to reach the pool below; it requires a careful walk down a narrow, rock-hewn trail with chain handles, but most reasonably dexterous people can handle it. The trail leads to the top the waterfalls and a high viewpoint.

Beaver Falls

Beaver Falls is another 2 miles (3.2 km) beyond Mooney Falls toward the river, which is 7 miles (11.3 km) from the campground.

Lower Navajo Falls (top); Beaver Falls (bottom)

Mooney Falls

These are not so much water falls as a series of white-and-blue cataracts. The falls are underwhelming compared to Havasu and Mooney, and for most it is not worth the very difficult hike here.

HIKING AND BACKPACKING

HAVASU CANYON TRAIL

DISTANCE: 8 miles (12.9 km) one-way to Supai Village; 10 miles (16.1 km) one-way to campground; 13 miles (20.9 kilometers) one-way to Beaver Falls
DURATION: 3-5 hours one-way
ELEVATION CHANGE: 2,000 feet (610 m)
EFFORT: Moderate
TRAILHEAD: Hualapai Hilltop

The hike to Havasu, Mooney, and Beaver Falls starts at the Hualapai Hilltop trailhead. From there, it's 8 miles (12.9 km) to the inner canyon village of **Supai,** where Havasupai Lodge, a tourism office, small café, and general store are located. For the first 2 miles (3.2 km) or so, rocky, moderately technical switchbacks lead to the canyon floor, a sandy bottomland where you're surrounded by eroded humps of seemingly melted, pockmarked sandstone.

When you reach the village, you'll see the twin rock spires, called **Wii'Gliva,** which tower over the little farms and homes of Supai. The trail continues 2 miles (3.2 km) to the campground, passing **Havasu Falls,** and then moves on to the Colorado River 7 miles (11.3 km) down the creek, passing **Mooney and Beaver Falls** and through a gorgeous green riparian stretch. The Havasupai Reservation ends at Beaver Falls, where Grand Canyon National Park begins.

It's difficult to hike from the village or the campground to the Colorado River in one day—it's a long, wet route with many creek crossings and not always easy to follow; plus, there's no camping allowed at the river, so you must make it back by bedtime. Only experienced, strong hikers should attempt the trek to the Colorado River and back.

There are no water stations or toilets along the trail. An ideal way to visit is to hike in and take the 10-minute helicopter out. It takes off from a lot in Supai between the tourism office and the café, and the helipad is only about 50 yards (46 m) from the Hualapai Hilltop trailhead parking lot.

backpacker hiking Havasu Canyon Trail

HAVASU CANYON FOOD OPTIONS

NAME	LOCATION	TYPE
Café at Supai Village	Supai Village	burgers, fry bread, Indian tacos

HAVASU CANYON CAMPGROUNDS

NAME	LOCATION	SEASON
Havasupai Campground	2 miles (3.2 km) from Supai Village between Havasu and Mooney Falls; hike-in only	year-round

FOOD

There are very few options for food if you're headed to Havasupai, where there's only a small café and a general store in Supai Village. Along Route 66, there are eateries at Grand Canyon Caverns and Seligman (page 174).

Indian taco made with fry bread

FOOD	PRICE	HOURS
café food	$5-10	8am-5pm daily

SITES AND AMENITIES	RV LIMIT	PRICE	RESERVATIONS
space for 300 people; toilets; potable water	n/a	$25	reservations are required to camp (www.havasupaireservations.com), but spots are first-come, first-served

BEST PICNIC SPOTS
Along the Havasu Canyon Trail

Even though those world-famous waterfalls await, don't hurry over lunch along the 8-mile (12.9-km) one-way hike to Supai from Hualapai Hill. One of the easier routes into the canyon, there are many beautiful spots along the trail that appear to have been designed from ancient times for trailside picnicking.

Near Havasu Falls

Roll out a blanket on the sandy banks or pick one of the picnic tables here and feel the spray of Havasu Falls as you dine.

You can picnic on the sands of Havasu falls.

HAVASU CANYON LODGING

NAME	LOCATION
Hualapai Lodge	Peach Springs
Caverns Inn	Grand Canyon Caverns, Historic Route 66, mile marker 115
Supai Motel	134 W. Chino St., Seligman
Historic Route 66 Motel	22750 W. Route 66, Seligman
Canyon Lodge	114 E. Chino St., Seligman
Havasupai Lodge	Supai Village (accessible only by foot, mule ride, or helicopter)

CAMPING

Reservations

To make a reservation to camp at the Havasupai campground near Havasu Falls, you have to reserve a space online at www.havasupaires-ervations.com beginning at 8am on February 1 of the year you want to go. Camping permits sell out fast, and it's not easy to get reservations.

Tips

The campground here is spread out along the creek about 2 miles (3.2 km) from the Supai Village. It's tempting to stop and jump in the water before you reach the campground, but to get a good spot you should set up first before hitting the water.

the campground along Havasu Creek

SEASON	OPTIONS	PRICE
year-round	hotel rooms	rooms starting at $150
year-round	motel rooms	rooms starting at $117
year-round	motel rooms	rooms starting at $69
year-round	motel rooms	rooms starting at $69
year-round	hotel rooms	rooms starting at $70
year-round	hotel rooms	rooms starting at $175

LODGING

Reservations and Tips

The Havasupai tribe requires that you stay overnight and have a reservation to visit Supai and the falls. Most visitors camp, but to stay at the **Havasupai Lodge** (www.havasupaireservations.com), make reservations far in advance.

Before hiking into Havasupai Lodge or the campground, most visitors stay the night at one of the motels along Historic Route 66 (page 176) to get an early start, especially during the summer. The closest hotels to the trailhead are the **Caverns Inn** and the **Hualapai Lodge** in Peach Springs. You'll find cheaper accommodations in **Seligman,** where there are several small, locally owned motels.

mules carrying goods on the way to Supai Village

Supai Motel in Seligman

INFORMATION AND SERVICES

Peach Springs, the Hualapai Reservation's capital, and where all the services in the Grand Canyon West area are located, is the closest town to Havasupai. There are very few services offered at Supai Village; hikers experiencing a health emergency will need to secure a helicopter ride.

Havasupai Tourism Office

160 Main St., Supai; tel. 928/448-2180; irregular hours

There is a small tourism office in the village of Supai. Hikers should stop here for a permit check on their way to the campground.

TRANSPORTATION

Getting There

From the South Rim

To reach Havasu Canyon and its waterfalls from the South Rim, you need to first reach the trailhead at Hualapai Hilltop. From the South Rim, take AZ 64 south to I-40, and then head west to the Ash Fork exit for Route 66. Drive west on the Mother Road, passing through Seligman. About 30 miles (48 km) past Seligman, turn north on Indian Route 18, and drive 60 miles (97 km) north to a parking area at Hualapai Hilltop, where the trailhead for Havasu Canyon is located. The drive from the South Rim to Hualapai Hilltop is 195 miles (315 km) total and takes about four hours.

From there, it's a moderate 8-mile (12.9-km) hike in to **Supai Village** and the lodge, and another 2 miles (3.2 km) to the campground. If you don't want to hike in, you can arrange to **rent a mule** (928/448-2121, 928/448-2174, or 928/448-2180; www.officialhavasupaitribe.com; $400 round-trip to campground) or take a 10-minute helicopter ride. **Airwest** (623/516-2790; 10am-1pm Sun.-Mon. and Thurs.-Fri. Mar. 15-Oct. 15, 10am-1pm Sun. and Fri. Oct. 16-Mar. 14; $85 one-way) operates helicopters that take off and land in Supai Village every 10 minutes or so in a lot between the tourism office and the café. At Hualapai Hilltop, the helipad is only about 50 yards (46 m) from the trailhead parking lot.

Gas

There is gas available all along **I-40** and at Ashfork, Seligman, and Peach Springs on **Old Route 66.**

desert bighorn sheep

BIRDS AND WILDLIFE

Across five distinct but ranging Grand Canyon plant communities (ponderosa pine forest, pinyon-juniper woodland, desert scrub, riparian, and mixed-conifer forest), predator and prey carry on the amoral game of survival. Some animals here are generalists willing to ignore borders and boundaries, while other niche-bound natives exist here, precariously, and nowhere else in the world.

CALIFORNIA CONDORS

The largest bird in North America, the California condor is a scavenger with a wingspan up to 9.5 feet (2.9 m). The bird almost went extinct in the 1980s but was saved from the brink and reintroduced to canyon country in 1997. Soon after they could be seen soaring and gliding over the South Rim near Grand Canyon Village. One theory is that the ancient scavengers are drawn to the busy South Rim because they have always followed herds.

Where to See Them

- **Grand Canyon Village** (page 44)

PEREGRINE FALCONS

Another near-extinct species that has come back strong in canyon country is the peregrine falcon, the fastest animal in the world with diving speeds up to 200 miles per hour (322 km/h). For nearly 30 years from the 1970s-late 1990s, the peregrine languished on the federal Endangered Species List, but scientists now estimate that there are about 100 pairs throughout the Grand Canyon. Look for a wingspan of up to 3.5 feet (1.1 m), a blue-gray "helmet" head, and a blue-gray back with a gray or tan underside and dark bars.

Where to See Them

- **Pipe Creek Vista** (page 61)

RED-TAILED HAWKS

Fairly common in canyon country and Northern Arizona, the red-tailed hawk is a year-round resident of the Grand Canyon and can be seen soaring and hunting over the gorge and nesting in the trees and along cliff edges on both rims. Raptors are often difficult to identify unless they are sitting still, so it's helpful to learn what they look like in flight. The red-tailed hawk has a 4-foot (1.2-m) wingspan, a reddish-brown tail, and

California condor

in flight has broad rounded wings and a short wide tail.

Where to See Them

- **Pipe Creek Vista** (page 61)
- **Bright Angel Point** (page 89)
- **Cape Royal Road** (page 95)

SQUIRRELS

The South Rim has the **Abert's squirrel,** a common gray-and-white resident that hangs around the Rim Trail and the viewpoints. You likely won't be walking on the trail long before you see one of these adorable creatures scurrying around, looking for dropped scraps. Take a picture but do not feed.

On the North Rim there is the one-of-a-kind **Kaibab squirrel,** of a dark-brown or even black hue, which occurs nowhere else in the world. These two cousins were once the same species but they split after being separated and isolated long, long ago by the vast and confusing impediment of the Grand Canyon between them.

Where to See the Albert's Squirrel

- **Rim Trail** (page 56)

Where to See the Kaibab Squirrel

- **Cape Royal** (page 98)

DEER

Light-brown mule deer, with the distinctive big ears of the mules they resemble, range across the canyonlands and are the most visible mammal in the region. Mule deer can be seen all over Northern Arizona, even in residential areas

peregrine falcon (top); Kaibab squirrel (middle); deer (bottom)

and crossing busy highways. They generally hang around in small family groups chomping on bushes, including mothers with small fawns and young males with velvety antlers. They are easily identified by their large ears and black-tipped tails, and they typically grow to be about 3.5 feet (1.1 m) tall and about 7 feet (2.1 m) long. Find them on the South Rim, the North Rim, and in the inner canyon.

Where to See Them

- **Rim Trail** (page 56)
- **Transept Trail** (page 100)
- **Widforss Trail** (page 104)
- **Phantom Ranch** (page 149)
- **Indian Garden** (page 134)

ELK

Introduced to the Williams area in the early 1900s, the Rocky Mountain elk, a large ungulate, migrated to the South Rim. It is considered an invasive species, living off nonnative grasses and non-natural water sources, but it's still thrilling to see them in the park. Elk often hang around the forest along the main road to and from the South Entrance station, and excited people will sometimes stop in the middle of traffic to take pictures.

Where to See Them

- **South Entrance station** (page 74)

DESERT BIGHORN SHEEP

These usually elusive ungulates seem positively happy to see you if you happen to cross their path on the inner canyon trails. Dexterous,

elk (top); desert bighorn sheep (middle); short-horned lizard (bottom)

adorable, and fascinating, seeing a desert bighorn sheep is one of the joys of entering the inner canyon.

Where to See Them

• **River Trail** (page 140)

LIZARDS

Some 41 species of reptile are found throughout the canyon, including 18 different lizards. The **collared lizard** is by the far the most common; look for a small dinosaur with two black collars around the neck, a white belly, and large head. The males have bright green scales. You are most likely to see the **yellow-black spiny lizard,** which looks like its name suggests it would, inside the canyon. You probably won't see the **short-horned lizard** at all because its grayish camouflage keeps it hidden in plain sight.

Where to See Them

Look down everywhere you go in Arizona and the Southwest. In the morning and evening you will often see lizards perched on rocks doing push-ups, a common display of strength to defend territory.

SNAKES

Among the many snake species in the canyon there are six rattlesnake species, including the pinkish **Grand Canyon rattlesnake,** which occurs nowhere else.

Where to See Them

Hope that you don't! Snakes don't want you to see them, and if you do you should just leave them alone.

Grand Canyon rattlesnake

redwall limestone

GEOLOGIC STRATA

The Grand Canyon is something like a living book of deep-time history, with its geologic strata left open for all to see and each layer revealing the ancient environmental conditions of its formation. It's not a complete book; there are missing layers called "unconformities" that have eroded away to nothing. The layers that remain generally grow older as you descend into the canyon, with the oldest being the hot, black rock walls of the inner canyon.

HOW TO LEARN ABOUT THE CANYON'S LAYERS

Most of the Grand Canyon's striations are visible from the rim viewpoints if you look at the cliffs, but to learn more about them you'll have to dig deeper.

- The South Rim's **Yavapai Geology Museum** (page 41) is the best place in the park to learn about canyon geology. From here, stroll down the **Trail of Time** (page 44), each meter of which contains a marker that equals one million years.

- Take note: The best tool for properly viewing the canyon's geologic wonders is a good pair of **binoculars.**

- Finally, in case you were wondering, **overlooks** named for layers of strata (Toroweap Overlook, Coconino Overlook, etc.) generally sit on top of the layer for which they are named.

KAIBAB AND TOROWEAP FORMATIONS

Off-white (often described as creamy) mixed with yellow-gray, the Kaibab and Toroweap formations are about 270 million years old and form the rim's cap-rock, on which you might be standing now. They form roughly the top 500-700 feet (150-200 m). The Toroweap formation appears as pink beds below the Kaibab cliff. Though it can be seen from really anywhere on both rims—just look across the canyon and identify the top, cream-colored layer—the most dramatic and beautiful example is the amazing Angels Window on the North Rim, at the end of the Cape Royal Drive.

Where to See It

- **Angels Window** (page 91)

COCONINO SANDSTONE

About 275 million years old and composed of the remains of a great desert, the Coconino Sandstone is the white and buff-colored cliff below the Kaibab and Toroweap Formations, about 700 feet (213 m) below the rim. From the South Rim and North Rim, look at the cliff formations with the whiteish layer beneath the top approximately 700 feet (213 m). An easy way to identify the layers is to look at one of the named formations, such as 7,570-foot-high (2,307-m-high) **Shiva Temple,** which can be seen across the canyon from Hopi Point and other viewpoints along the Hermit Road. The striations are particularly identifiable in the layers of these monumental formations. The Coconino Sandstone is the cream-colored band below the Kaibab and Toroweap layers.

Where to See It

- **Hopi Point** (page 49)

HERMIT FORMATION

The Hermit Formation is a mixture of red sandstone, siltstone, and shale about 1,200 feet (366 m) thick. The top 300 feet (91 m) of this formation is a shale slope called **Hermit Shale,** which is about 280 million years old. The iron oxides in the Hermit Formation and the Supai Group cause most of the redness in the canyon walls.

From the viewpoints on the South Rim and North Rims, find the red shale slopes below the Coconino Sandstone. From the North Rim, look for the 7,851-foot (2,393-m) **Brahma Temple** formation from Bright Angel Point near the Grand Canyon Lodge. The Hermit layer forms the reddish slopes beneath the Coconino and Kaibab layers.

Where to See It

• **Bright Angel Point** (page 89)

SUPAI GROUP

About 285-315 million years old, the Supai Group is a thick layer of red sandstone and shale below the Hermit Formation that averages about 2,000 feet (610 m) thick. See examples on Supai Tunnel on the North Kaibab Trail, or by viewing a formation such Shiva Temple from Hopi Point or Brahma Temple from Bright Angel Point.

Where to See It

• **Supai Tunnel** (page 102)

• **Hopi Point** (page 49)

• **Bright Angel Point** (page 89)

REDWALL LIMESTONE

Redwall limestone makes up the reddish, 500-foot-high (152-m-high) cliff about halfway between the South Rim and the river, as well as many of the canyon's dramatic mesas and buttes. The limestone formation also has many caves, arches, and springs and was formed in a wide shallow

Kaibab Formation on South Rim (top); Toroweap Formation (middle); Hermit shale (bottom)

203

sea. Called Redwall, it's actually gray, but has been stained by iron oxides seeping down from the Supai Formation above it.

Look for Redwall Limestone from the South Rim viewpoints, on the high red cliffs about halfway between the river and rim

Where to See It

- **South Rim viewpoints** (page 41)

Temple Butte limestone
385 million years old

TRAIL OF TIME

Temple Butte limestone (top); Bright Angel shale (bottom)

TEMPLE BUTTE FORMATION

The Temple Butte is a lavender sea deposit below the Redwall that's about 385 million years old.

Where to See It

- **Desert View Drive viewpoints** (page 54)

MUAV LIMESTONE

A mixture of gray and greenish-gray sea-deposited limestone, the 505-million-year-old "lumpy" Mauv layer is about 400 feet (122 m) thick on average and has many caverns created by groundwater.

Where to See It

- **South Rim viewpoints** (page 41)

BRIGHT ANGEL SHALE

The greenish Bright Angel Shale, about 400 feet (122 m) thick on average, forms the **Tonto Plateau,** an easily recognizable platform above the inner canyon.

Where to See It

- **South Rim viewpoints** (page 41)

TAPEATS SANDSTONE

An average of about 200 feet (610 m) of thick, dark brown Tapeats Sandstone makes up the sheer cliffs below the Tonto Plateau, and sits on top of the Vishnu Group—although technically it shouldn't. Missing between these two layers is some 500 million years of geologic history, a long dark age geologists call the "Great Unconformity."

Where to See It

- **Bright Angel Trail** (page 58) below Indian Garden

GRAND CANYON SUPERGROUP

A large mixed group of shale, sandstone, and siltstone running horizontally, between 650-1,250 million years old and some 12,000 feet (4,000 m) thick.

Where to See It

- **South Kaibab Trail** (page 61)
- **North Kaibab Trail** (page 102)
- **Point Imperial** (page 89)
- **Cape Royal** (page 98)

Grand Canyon Supergroup

VISHNU BASEMENT ROCKS

The hot black walls of the inner canyon rise up to 1,500 feet (457 m) above the river, composed of metamorphic rock called the Vishnu Group, which is veined with lighter, even pink, shades of Zoroaster gneiss. Some 3,000 feet (914 m) below the South Rim, these are the Grand Canyon's oldest rocks at 1.7-1.8 billion years old.

Where to See It

- **Inner canyon** (page 119)
- **South Rim viewpoints** (page 41) (with binoculars)

Grand Canyon basement rocks

Kaibab Bridge (Black Bridge)

ESSENTIALS

GETTING THERE

AIR

Many travelers fly into Sky Harbor International Airport in Phoenix and then rent a car for the 225-mile (360-km), 4-hour drive north to the South Rim and environs. Many other canyon tourists drive or take bus tours west to the South Rim from Las Vegas, Nevada (280 mi/450 km, 5-hour drive), and from Los Angeles, California (494 mi/795 km, 7.5-hour drive). The closest airport to Grand Canyon National Park is in Flagstaff.

Phoenix Sky Harbor International Airport

PHX; 3400 E. Sky Harbor Blvd., Phoenix, AZ; 602/273-3300; www.skyharbor.com **DRIVING TIME TO GRAND CANYON:** 4 hours to South Entrance

McCarran International Airport (Las Vegas, NV)

LAS; 5757 Wayne Newton Blvd., Las Vegas, NV; 702/261-5211; www.mccarran.com **DRIVING TIME TO GRAND CANYON:** 5 hours to South Entrance; 2.5 hours to Grand Canyon West

Flagstaff Pullam Airport

FLG; Flagstaff, AZ; 928/556-1234; www.flagstaff.az.gov **DRIVING TIME TO GRAND CANYON:** 1.5 hours to South Entrance; 2 hours to East Entrance; 4 hours to North Entrance

Los Angeles International Airport

LAX; 1 World Way, Los Angeles, CA; 855/463-5252; www.flylax.com **DRIVING TIME TO GRAND CANYON:** 7.5 hours to South Entrance

CAR

Most Grand Canyon National Park visitors reach the South Rim from either Flagstaff or Williams, and enter the park through the **South Entrance** on AZ 64. It's the park's busiest entrance by far; during the summer there's likely to be a long line at the South Entrance, especially on weekends and holidays. (A smart way to skip these lines is to leave your car at the IMAX theater in Tusayan (a small settlement of hotels and restaurants just outside the park gates), purchase a pass there, and then hop on the free shuttle bus into the park.) From the South Entrance you're just minutes away from prime parking spots, the Grand Canyon Visitor Center, and Grand Canyon Village.

Reached by taking U.S. 89 north from Flagstaff to Cameron and then heading west on AZ 64, the **East Entrance** receives much less traffic. The eastern route enters the park at the Desert View section, about an hour's scenic drive from Grand Canyon Village and the main visitor center.

Road Conditions and Closures

The South and East Entrances are open year-round, but the road leading to the North Entrance, AZ 67, closes December-mid-May. Call 928/638-7496 for an up-to-date recording on current road conditions in and around the park.

Driving Times

The Grand Canyon is often included in longer trips around the southwestern states.

- **Zion National Park:** 2.5 hours to North Entrance (closed Dec.-May)

- **Monument Valley:** 3.5 hours to East Entrance

- **From Albuquerque:** 6 hours to South Entrance

FAST FACTS

- **Park established:** 1919
- **Park visitation in 2019:** 5,974,411
- **Park area:** 1,904 square miles (4,931 square km)

TRAIN

The **Grand Canyon Railway** (800/843-8724; www.thetrain.com) runs daily between the Williams station and the South Rim depot in Grand Canyon Village, with several different ticket levels ($67-226 adults, $32-153 children 2-15).

The **Amtrak Southwest Chief route** (800/872-7245; www.amtrak.com), which mirrors the old Santa Fe Railroad's *Super Chief* route of the grand Fred Harvey days, stops twice daily (one eastbound, one westbound) at Flagstaff's classic **downtown depot** (1 E. Route 66), the former Santa Fe headquarters and also the town's visitor center. The route crosses the country from Chicago to L.A., dipping into the Southwest through northern New Mexico and northern Arizona. Amtrak provides bus service from the Flagstaff Depot to Williams for those with tickets for the Grand Canyon Railroad. When you are booking your Amtrak ticket, make sure to choose Grand Canyon Railway Depot as your final destination rather than Flagstaff.

BUS

The **Phoenix Greyhound bus station** (2115 E. Buckeye Rd.; 602/389-4200; www.greyhound.com) is located near Sky Harbor International Airport. The closest Greyhound bus station to Grand Canyon is the one in **Flagstaff** (880 E Butler Ave.; 928/774-4573; www.greyhound.com).

Groome Transportation aka Arizona Shuttle (928/350-8466, https://groometransportation.com) offers several daily round-trip shuttles between Phoenix's Sky Harbor Airport and Flagstaff's Amtrak depot ($48 pp one-way). Groome also offers shuttles between Flagstaff and Grand Canyon National Park (Mar.-Oct.; $60 round-trip for adults).

PARK ENTRY
Fees and Passes

The **entrance fee** for Grand Canyon National Park is $35 for a private vehicle with up to 15 people. The pass is good on both the South and North Rims for seven consecutive days. Motorcyclists pay $30 to enter, and those walking, cycling, or riding the free Purple Route shuttle bus from Tusayan or the Grand Canyon Railway from Williams, or who are part of a tour group, pay $20.

You can purchase a digital entrance pass at www.recreation.gov and https://yourpassnow.com, or pick one up on your way to the park at the **Williams-Kaibab National Forest Visitor Center** (200 W. Railroad Ave., Williams; 928/635-1418 or 800/863-0546; 8am-6:30pm daily spring-summer, 8am-5pm daily fall-winter), the **Flagstaff Visitor Center** (1 E. Route 66, Flagstaff; 928/774-9541 or 800/379-0065; www.flagstaffarizona.org; 8am-5pm Mon.-Sat., 9am-4pm Sun.), or the **Grand Canyon Visitor Center** (Rte. 64, Tusayan; 928/638-2468; www.explorethecanyon.com; 8am-10pm daily Mar.-Oct., 10am-8pm daily Nov.-Feb.).

Annual and lifetime entry passes include:

- **Grand Canyon National Park Annual Pass:** $70; valid for entry to Grand Canyon National Park for 12 months from the date of purchase.

- **America the Beautiful Annual Pass:** $80; valid for entry to all National Parks and federal recreational lands that charge an entrance fee for 12 months from the date of purchase.

- **America the Beautiful Senior Pass:** Lifetime $80, annual $20: available to U.S. citizens or permanent residents 62 and up, valid for entry to all National Parks and federal recreational lands that charge an entrance fee.

Entrance Stations

Grand Canyon National Park has three entrance stations:

- **South Entrance** (AZ 64): most popular (and crowded) entrance to the park; closest entrance to the main Grand Canyon Visitor Center and Grand Canyon Village.

- **East Entrance** (AZ 64): enters the park at the Desert View section, one-hour drive to Grand Canyon Village.

- **North Rim Entrance** (AZ 67): access to the North Rim; closed December-mid-May.

GETTING AROUND

DRIVING

Driving to, around, and inside Grand Canyon National Park's busy **South Rim** section can be challenging, especially in the summer when the park is at its busiest. Some six million visitors come here every year, and most of them travel in cars. During the high season most of the parking lots near Grand Canyon Visitor Center and in Grand Canyon Village fill up by 10am. Arrive before 9am or after 4pm to secure the best parking spots.

Driving from sight to sight in your own vehicle is not the ideal way to visit the park. This strategy works better during the winter months when the **Hermit Road,** which leads to nine viewpoints on the western end of the park, is open to cars. From March to November, the 7-mile (11.3-km) one-way scenic road is open only to shuttle buses, bicycles, and pedestrians.

You will need your own car to travel to the park's **Desert View** section, about an hour's drive from Grand Canyon Village on the park's eastern edge, as the shuttle buses only go as far as the Yaki Point and the South Kaibab Trailhead.

While driving in and around the park, keep a careful lookout for wildlife, especially along AZ 64 just outside the South Entrance. Inside the park, drive slowly and watch for pedestrians and bicycles.

TRAVELING BY RV

The South Rim's in-park RV campground, **Trailer Village** (877/404-4611; www.visitgrandcanyon.com), is about a 0.5 mile (0.8 km) from Mather Campground and right near Market Plaza. Open year-round, it has full hookups and pull-throughs for vehicles up to 50 feet (15.2 m) long. Reservations are a must during high season. There are no in-park RV-only campgrounds on the North Rim. You can park a rig of up to 40 feet (12.2 m) combined vehicle length at the North Rim campground, but there are no hookups. There is a dump and water station. The closest RV park with full hookups is Kaibab Camper Village, about 45 miles (72.4 m) from the rim near Jacob Lake. On both rims, most of the parking lots have dedicated RV spots.

SHUTTLES
South Rim

Grand Canyon National Park's South Rim has a fleet of buses that run on natural gas. Operated by friendly and knowledgeable drivers, these shuttle buses crisscross the park all day and into the night, taking passengers to various viewpoints and sights for free. During the high season there may be long lines at the many shuttle stops throughout the park, but it is still the best strategy for getting around. The shuttle buses run every 10-30 minutes, beginning about an hour before sunrise and stopping about an hour after sunset.

Tusayan Route

You also have the option to leave your vehicle outside the park's South Entrance in the small town of Tusayan. The shuttle's free Tusayan Route (Purple) runs from early spring-fall, allowing you to leave your car behind, skip the long entrance lines, and head straight for the main Grand Canyon Visitor Center without worrying about finding parking. The shuttle runs every 20 minutes and takes about 20 minutes from Tusayan to the visitor center inside the park. It stops at the IMAX Theater, the Best Western Grand Canyon Squire Inn, and the Grand Hotel, all of which have large parking lots. You must have your park entrance pass before you board the shuttle; you can buy one at various places in Tusayan. The best place to buy an entrance pass, park your car, and hop on the shuttle is at the **Grand Canyon Visitor Center and IMAX Theater** (unless you are staying at one of the hotels mentioned above). You can also buy an entrance pass at www.recreation.gov.

Trans-Canyon Shuttle

928/638-2820; www.trans-canyonshuttle.com; $90 one-way; reservations required

The Trans-Canyon Shuttle makes a daily round-trip excursion between the North and South Rims, departing the North Rim at 7am and arriving at the South Rim at 11:30am. The shuttle then leaves the South Rim at 1:30pm and arrives back at the North Rim at 6pm. During the high season (spring and summer), the shuttle runs twice daily from the South Rim to the North Rim (8am-12:30pm and 1:30pm-6pm) and twice daily from the North Rim to the South Rim (7am-11:30am and 2pm-6:30pm).

NEARBY TOWNS

NEAR THE SOUTH ENTRANCE

Tusayan

About 1 mile (1.6 km) south of the park's South Entrance, the town of Tusayan is the closest gateway town outside the park. It makes for a decent stop if you're hungry. A lot of tour buses stop here, so you might find yourself crowded into waiting for a table at some places, especially during the summer high season. A number of accommodations line AZ 64 in the town (https://grandcanyoncvb.org). There is also a year-round RV park, **Grand Canyon Camper Village** (549 Camper Village Ln., Tusayan; 928/638-2887; www.grandcanyoncampervillage.com).

The town is also the home of the (non-NPS-affiliated) **Grand Canyon Visitor Center** (Rte. 64; 928/638-2468; www.explorethecanyon.com; 8am-10pm daily Mar.-Oct., 10am-8pm daily Nov.-Feb.), which has been a popular first stop for park visitors since the 1980s. You can purchase a park pass here, book tours, and check out some displays about the canyon, but the center wouldn't be worth the stop if not for its IMAX Theater. You can also leave your car here and hop on the **free shuttle bus (Tusayan Route/Purple Line)** to the park.

Biking into Grand Canyon National Park is relatively easy from Tusayan, via the Tusayan Greenway, a 6.5-mile (10.5-km) one-way paved bike trail. There is parking at the trailhead (make a left at the traffic circle north of the Grand Canyon Visitor Center), and the shuttle bus can accommodate your bike, if you prefer to ride it back to town (or vice-versa).

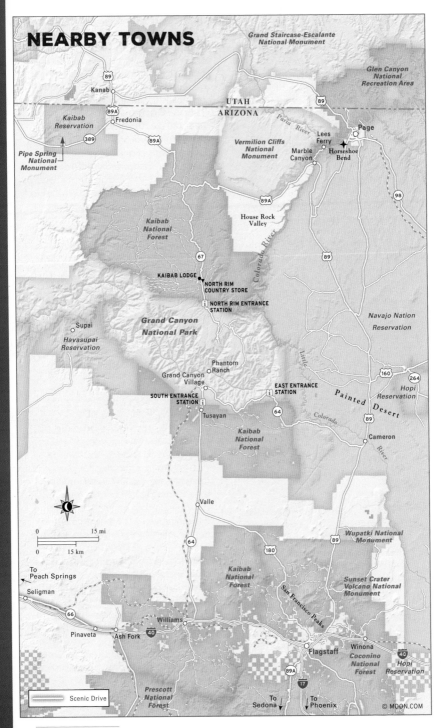

NEARBY TOWNS

Grand Staircase-Escalante
National Monument

Glen Canyon
National
Recreation Area

Kanab

89

UTAH
ARIZONA

89

Kaibab
Reservation

89A

Fredonia

Paria River

Lees
Ferry

Page

Pipe Spring
National
Monument

389

89A

Vermilion Cliffs
National
Monument

Marble
Canyon

Horseshoe
Bend

98

House Rock
Valley

89A

Kaibab
National
Forest

67

Colorado River

89

KAIBAB LODGE

NORTH RIM
COUNTRY STORE

Navajo Nation
Reservation

NORTH RIM ENTRANCE
STATION

Supai

Grand Canyon
National Park

Little

Havasupai
Reservation

Phantom
Ranch

Grand Canyon
Village

160

264

EAST ENTRANCE
STATION

Painted

Hopi
Reservation

SOUTH ENTRANCE
STATION

Colorado

Desert

89

Tusayan

64

Cameron

River

Valle

Wupatki National
Monument

To Peach Springs

0   15 mi

0   15 km

64

180

89

Seligman

Kaibab
National
Forest

Sunset Crater
Volcano National
Monument

66

San Francisco Peaks

Williams

Winona

Coconino
National
Forest

Hopi
Reservation

Pinaveta

Ash Fork

40

40

Flagstaff

89A

17

Prescott
National
Forest

To
Sedona

To
Phoenix

© MOON.COM

Scenic Drive

Williams

This small, historic town along I-40 (what used to be Route 66) is only an hour's drive along AZ 64 from the South Rim. Though much smaller than Flagstaff, Williams is a popular tourist area with many excellent hotels, motels, and restaurants, and it is the best place to base your visit if you plan to ride the Grand Canyon Railway into and out of the park. Williams has some of the most affordable independent accommodations in the Grand Canyon region, as well as several chain hotels.

Stop at the **Williams-Kaibab National Forest Visitor Center** (200 W. Railroad Ave.; 928/635-4061; www.fs.usda.gov/main/kaibab/home; 8am-6:30pm daily spring-summer, 8am-5pm daily fall-winter) for information about food, lodging, and more in Williams, the Grand Canyon, and camping and hiking in the Kaibab National Forest.

Flagstaff

Located 80 scenic miles (129 km) southeast of the South Entrance, a 1.5-hour drive, Flagstaff is the largest city near the canyon and the capital of the Colorado Plateau. It has the most diverse restaurants and accommodations in the region. Most river trips will convene at a prearranged hotel in Flagstaff before moving on to launch at Lees Ferry.

FOOD

Flagstaff has a fairly sophisticated restaurant scene, with places serving cuisines from all over the world as well as creative and inspired American fare. Downtown (stretching northeast from Route 66 between Humphreys and San Francisco Streets) and the Southside Historic District (south of the railroad tracks from downtown) have the best local eateries, including many dedicated to sustainability and using locally and regionally sourced ingredients.

ACCOMMODATIONS

Being an interstate town close to several world-renowned sights, Flagstaff has all the chain hotels. A good value and a unique experience can be had at one of the historic downtown hotels. Along Route 66 as you enter town from the east, there are a large number of chain and locally owned small hotels and motels, including several old-school motor inns, and a few places that are likely inexpensive for a reason. East Flagstaff, while it lacks the charm of the downtown area, is an acceptable place to stay if you're just passing through. If you're a budget traveler and don't mind the hostel crowd, try the hostels in Flagstaff's Southside Historic District.

INFORMATION

The **Flagstaff Visitor Center** (1 E. Route 66; 928/774-9541 or 800/379-0065; www.flagstaffarizona.org; 8am-5pm Mon.-Sat., 9am-4pm Sun.), located in the old train depot in the center of town, has all kinds of information on Flagstaff and the surrounding area.

NEAR THE EAST ENTRANCE

Cameron

HISTORIC CAMERON TRADING POST AND LODGE

800/338-7385; www.camerontradingpost.com

Established in 1916, Historic Cameron Trading Post and Lodge is a busy travel center in the western section of the Navajo Nation, about 30 miles (48 km) east of Grand Canyon National Park's Desert View section, at the junction of AZ 64 and U.S. 89. The stone and log complex has served the region as a trading post, hotel, restaurant, art gallery, and general oasis of civilization—it's hard not to stop here if you're traveling through Navajoland north of Flagstaff.

With its professionally prepared, native-inspired cuisine, the **restaurant** (6am-9:30pm daily summer, 7am-9pm daily winter) here is one of the best in the region, with delicious Navajo, Mexican, and American dishes served in a dining room with a stone fireplace and Navajo rugs on the walls.

The **lodge** (rooms starting at $79), which has been expanded and remodeled over the years, makes a perfect base for a visit to the Grand Canyon, Indian Country, Lake Powell, and the Arizona Strip. There's also an RV park ($35 full hookups; no bathroom or showers).

NEAR THE NORTH ENTRANCE

Kaibab Lodge

5 mi/8 km north of park entrance at AZ 67, mile marker 605; 928/638-2389; mid-May-mid-Oct.

Tucked along the tree line on the edge of an expansive green meadow, 18 miles (29 km) from the rim and 16 miles (26 km) from the North Kaibab Trailhead, the Kaibab Lodge is a rustic wilderness haven that's been welcoming North Rim wanderers since the late 1920s. There are a variety of cabins and motel-style rooms (starting at $100)—some are ADA accessible—and all have private bathrooms. There are no TVs here, no Wi-Fi, and cell phones don't work. The lodge serves breakfast ($6-12) and dinner ($11-30)—burgers, pasta, ribs, steaks, etc.—daily mid-May-mid-October.

Across AZ 67 from the lodge is the only convenience store within 100 miles (161 km), the **North Rim Country Store** (AZ 67, mile marker 605, 18 mi/29 km north of the rim; 928/638-2383; www.northrimcountrystore.com; 7am-7pm daily mid-May-late Oct.). It also sells gas, vehicle supplies, and souvenirs.

Page

Page, about 2.5 hours from both the South and North Rims, is a good base for those visiting both rims, as well as nearby Lake Powell and Glen Canyon National Recreation Area. While surrounded by stark sandstone beauty, Page has little to recommend itself other than its easy chain hotels and restaurants.

FOOD AND ACCOMMODATIONS

Millions of tourists drive through Page every season, and as a result the area has all the usual chain hotels and several chain restaurants—more than is usual for a small town in the middle of nowhere. You'll find most of Page's services along Lake Powell Boulevard, the main drag through town.

INFORMATION

The **Page Lake Powell Tourism Bureau** (647-A Elm St.; 928/660-3405; www.visitpagelakepowell.com) has all kinds of information on Page, Glen Canyon, and the rest of the region, and the staff there can help you book tours. The bureau runs the **Visitor Information Center** (10am-4pm Mon.-Fri., 10am-2pm Sat.), located inside the Powell Museum (6 N. Lake Powell Blvd.).

Kanab, Utah

About an hour's drive west from Page and 7 miles (11.3 km) north of the Arizona border along U.S. 89A in Utah is Kanab, a tiny, rural burg, far from the real world. Isolated out here on the western end of the Colorado Plateau, the town is home to only about 4,000 year-round residents. It is nonetheless well set up for travelers and tourists. Kanab is a great choice if you're wrapping a trip to Zion and Bryce Canyon National Parks (40 mi/64 km to the northwest and 77 mi/124 km to the northeast, respectively) along with your visit to Grand Canyon, or if you're just visiting the North Rim, which is just 80 miles (129 km) or about 1.5 hours away.

Here you'll find varied accommodations, including several chain hotels and restaurants, although a few unique choices are available as well, most of them spread out along the main drag. For more information about Kanab's offerings, seek out the **Kane County Visitor Information Center** (78 South 100 East; 435/644-5033; https://visitsouthernutah.com; 8am-5pm Mon.-Fri., 9am-5pm Sat. and holidays, 11am-5pm Sun. summer).

RECREATION

A trip to the Grand Canyon is almost necessarily an active one filled with fresh air and outdoor recreation. It's best to go to the park prepared to do some hiking, or at least a bit more walking than you would typically do in regular life. While hiking is by far the most popular activity at the canyon, bicycling around the park is becoming increasingly popular, and backpacking into the great gorge is still the reason Grand Canyon exists for a relatively small but growing and passionate subset of park visitors.

HIKING

Day hiking at Grand Canyon National Park includes everything from strolls along the flat and paved Rim Trail to all-day rim-to-rim marches. For most hikers, sticking to one of the corridor trails and under 6 miles (9.7 km) or less round-trip will ensure a memorable but safe outing that's relatively easy to accomplish. Beginning hikers and families with young children should consider a short hike of just 1-2 miles (1.6-2.3 km) round-trip with a specific destination.

Rules of the Trail

Never go off the trails or take shortcuts, and don't harass wildlife or take away artifacts, rocks, or items of any kind, whether natural or human-made.

RIGHT OF WAY

Hikers going up out of the canyon have the right-of-way; step aside and let them pass if you are heading down. Mule trains along the South Kaibab and North Kaibab Trails have the right-of-way whether they are headed up or down. Step aside and let the entire group pass before entering the trail again.

WARNINGS

Perhaps the most important rule of the trail in Grand Canyon is to take seriously the warnings that the National Park Service is ever at pains to impart via signs at trailheads and all around the park. These are simple and stark: Don't hike unprepared and don't underestimate the canyon's steep, rocky trails and desert environment. Hikers who are legendary in more familiar, less challenging country and climes could be in for a shock once they get a few miles down. And, as the Park Service often points out, just because you are young, healthy, and in prime physical shape doesn't mean you can take preparation for granted. Grand Canyon is different. Many have died after failing to learn this lesson, or after willfully ignoring it. Much of the trouble that hikers get into, it seems, is rooted in the massive public delusion that summer is the best season to hike Grand Canyon. Summer is the worst time to be a hiker below the rim. If you hike down into the canyon in the summer, you'll want to be off the trail by about 10am-11am to avoid the deadly heat, and wait until the relative cool of early evening before moving on again.

What to Wear

In all seasons, it's best to take a layered approach and to emphasize comfort over the long term. Winter hiking demands a lightweight but warm coat that stuffs small into your daypack, at least two more layers including a thermal base, and flexible, warm gloves. In summer, wear a long-sleeved shirt and, preferably, long hiking-style pants that ward off ultraviolet rays and dry quickly. Wear a hat that shades your face and a bandanna that protects your neck from the sun. Your hiking shoes should be well worn and comfortably your own before starting down the trail.

What to Take

A small backpack filled with water and salty, fatty snacks is the minimum you should carry on a day hike into Grand Canyon. And while you should never overload yourself, a few other lightweight items—such as a first-aid kit, headlamp, compass, and lighter—might come in handy in an emergency. If you're not sure how much water to take on your day hike, ask a ranger for advice. A lot of hikers in Grand Canyon use hiking poles; these are great for keeping your balance and hefting yourself up the trail, but hikers with arthritis in their hands may find them too painful to use. In winter and early spring the trails into the canyon are often icy and muddy. In icy conditions, take crampons along.

BACKPACKING

Just a small percentage of Grand Canyon visitors spend a night or two below the rim, most of them at only a few developed campgrounds along the **corridor trails—Bright Angel, South Kaibab,** and **North Kaibab Trails.** A fraction of that small percentage dares to venture beyond the main trails into the far backcountry scattered with primitive campsites. That said, it's fairly easy to launch a backpacking expedition into the heart of the canyon and spend the night on the banks of Bright Angel Creek. A popular way to visit the inner canyon is to backpack from rim to rim, starting at the South Rim and ending at the North Rim (or the other way around), and camping for one, two, or even three nights along the way. Perhaps the most popular, time-honored Grand Canyon backpacking trip is a few nights at Bright Angel Campground near the Colorado River and Phantom Ranch, hiking in and out via the South Kaibab Trail, the Bright Angel Trail, or both.

Backcountry Permits

All overnight backpacking trips into Grand Canyon require a **backcountry permit** ($10 plus $8 pp per night), and they are not always easy to obtain. You must plan your trip carefully and follow the park's strict guidelines for applying, and there is no guarantee that you will be successful. Camping below the rim at any of the corridor campgrounds is limited to two consecutive nights March 1-November 14; you can stay for up to four consecutive nights November 15-February 28. You have a better chance of obtaining a permit for groups of fewer than seven people. In the more remote sites, you can stay up to seven consecutive nights in a particular backcountry use area.

WHEN TO APPLY

You can apply for a permit 10 days before the first of the month that is four months before your hike. So, for hikes starting in, say, January, get your permit request in between August 20-September 1 by 5pm. It doesn't matter which day you turn it in; it just has to be there between the dates to receive "Earliest Consideration" status, to which the rangers give equal and random attention. Similarly, for hikes in September, apply between April 20-May 1; for August, apply between March 20-April 1, and so on (there's a handy schedule on the park's website). Expect to hear back within about three weeks.

HOW TO APPLY

Go to the **park's website** (www.nps. gov/grca), print out a backcountry permit request form, fill it out, and then **fax** (928/638-2125) it first thing in the morning on the date in question—so, if you want to hike in October (one of the best months to be below the rim), you would fax your request May 20-June 1. On the first day of the month the fax number is usually busy throughout the day. On the permit request form you'll indicate at which campgrounds you plan to stay. The permit is your reservation. For more information on obtaining a backcountry permit, call the **Backcountry Information Center** (928/638-7875; 8am-noon and 1pm-5pm daily).

IN-PERSON AND LAST-MINUTE PERMITS

Rangers don't consider **in-person permit requests** until three months before the date of the hike—for example, if you want to hike in October, you can't apply for a permit in person until

DARK SKIES

Grand Canyon National Park has been named a "Dark Sky" park by the International Dark-Sky Association, making it a prime spot for stargazing and sky-watching. The canyon's remote, rural location is largely free of serious light pollution, and a long-term project to tone down some 5,000 light fixtures throughout the park has taken the darkness here to another level.

SKY-WATCHING SPOTS

On clear nights the viewpoints along the **Hermit Road** and **Desert View Drive** (both on the South Rim) are great places to set up a telescope. Also ask the rangers at the visitor center for suggestions. On the North Rim, good places to set up a telescope include the porch of **Grand Canyon Lodge** and **Bright Angel Point.**

ASTRONOMY PROGRAMS

In late June join the Tucson Amateur Astronomy Association at the South Rim for the annual **Star Party** (www.tucsonastronomy.org, free)—eight days of viewing the dark night skies over the canyonlands, scanning for planets and galaxies, and mingling with starry-eyed astronomers from around the world. During the event, park rangers offer constellation walks every night at 9pm, 9:30pm, and 10pm.

July 1, when most if not all of the permits for that month will have likely been issued. However, there is a way to obtain **last-minute permits** to hike into the canyon if you have the flexibility and money to stay in the park for a few days and hike on short notice. Last-minute permits are available only for corridor campgrounds—Indian Garden, Bright Angel, and Cottonwood—and are for one or two consecutive nights. To try for a last-minute permit, head over to the Backcountry Information Center between 8am-noon and 1pm-5pm and request a wait-list number. This determines your place in line the following morning at 8am, and when your number is called you request the permit.

There are backcountry offices on both the South Rim and the North Rim:

- **South Rim Backcountry Information Center:** 1 Backcountry Rd., Grand Canyon Village; 928/638-7875; 8am-noon and 1pm-5pm daily

- **North Rim Backcountry Information Center:** North Rim Administration Bldg.; 8am-noon and 1pm-5pm daily May 15-Oct. 15

BIKING

Bikes are allowed on greenways and most roads throughout Grand Canyon National Park. However, bikes are not permitted below the rim or on hiking trails within the park, with the exception of the South Rim's **Hermit Road Greenway Trail** (a section of the Rim Trail—and about as close as you can get to the rim on a bike) and the North Rim's **Bridle Trail.**

Mountain Biking

Mountain bikes are not allowed on the trails inside the Grand Canyon. On the North Rim, try the rough road to **Point**

Sublime as a mountain bike trail within the park boundaries.

Road Biking

There are several roads in and around Grand Canyon National Park that make memorable and stunningly scenic road-bike rides. Very few of the roads outside the towns in this region have bike lanes, and the roads and highways leading into and around the park have little in the way of safe shoulders. The best bike rides around the canyon include **Desert View Drive** and **Hermit Road** on the South Rim and **AZ 67** from Jacob Lake to the North Rim.

All of the South Rim's hotels, stores, restaurants, and most of the viewpoints now have bike racks, so it's easy to stop and explore. Don't forget your lock.

FISHING

You must have a valid Arizona fishing license from the **Arizona Game & Fish Department** (602/942-3000; www.azgfd.com; $55 nonresidents, $37 residents) to fish in the Colorado River, where you'll find trout, striped and largemouth bass, catfish, and other species.

RAFTING

There are 16 approved outfitters offering rafting trips on the Colorado River through Grand Canyon National Park (www.gcroa.org). These companies offer 3- to 18-day river trips, the shorter ones starting at Lees Ferry and ending near Phantom Ranch, and the longer ones taking on 226 river miles (364 km) from Lees Ferry to Diamond Creek. About 75 percent of river-trippers choose a motorized boat, but you can also head downriver on an oar- or paddle-powered craft. Depending on the length of your trip, you may be required to hike into or out of the canyon about 10 miles (16.1 km) on the Bright Angel Trail.

The rafting season runs from late April-mid-September. The best times to go are in April, May, early June, and September. June-August the river corridor is very, very hot. It's a good idea to start planning and training for your river trip about a year out. Reservations should be made at least six months in advance if possible, though many of the approved outfitters will work with you and try to find a trip for you no matter when you call. The outfitters generally won't take children younger than 8 years old on motorized trips, or children under 12 years old on oar and paddle trips. And while there is no upper age limit, you need to be in relatively good shape to enjoy such a rugged adventure—able to at least hike 10 miles (16.1 km) into or out of the Grand Canyon. If you're just looking for one fun day riding the Colorado River's rapids, check out **Hualapai River Runners** at Grand Canyon West, outside the National Park. Hualapai River Runners will pick you up in Peach Springs (a 2-hour drive from the South Rim) and take you rafting through the Hualapai Nation via Diamond Creek Road (https://grandcanyonwest.com/explore/colorado-river-rafting/). Outfitters upriver at **Glen Canyon National Recreation Area** (about 1.5 hours from the South Rim) offer guided half-day smooth river rafting trips beyond the Glen Canyon Dam and around Horseshoe Bend on a motorized raft (riveradventures.com).

PARK TOURS

BUS TOURS
XANTERRA
303/297-2757 or 888/297-2757;
www.grandcanyonlodges.com
Throughout the year Xanterra, the company that runs most of the hotels and restaurants on the South Rim, offers various motorcoach tours within the park. Options include sunrise and sunset tours and longer drives to the eastern Desert View area and the western reaches of the park at Hermit's Rest. Typically done in vans or large, comfortable buses, these tours are generally fun and informative. The best tour offered is of the Desert View section of the park. It's the only section that's not accessible by free shuttle bus, and if you don't want to take your own vehicle to the eastern edges, it's the only way to get there.

MULE TOURS
XANTERRA CANYON
VISTAS MULE RIDE
303/297-2757 or 888/297-2757;
www.grandcanyonlodges.com
Park concessionaire Xanterra's Canyon Vistas Mule Ride along the South Rim goes year-round and includes one hour of orientation and a two-hour ride. Xanterra also offers overnight mule trips below the rim to Phantom Ranch.

GRAND CANYON TRAIL RIDES
On the North Rim, Grand Canyon Trail Rides offers three daily options during the high season: a one-hour trail ride through the forest and along the rim; a three-hour trail ride along the rim to Uncle Jim's Point; and a three-hour trail ride down the North Kaibab Trail to Supai Tunnel.

RANGER PROGRAMS

A schedule of ranger programs can be found online at go.nps.gov/gc_programs. During the high season South Rim ranger programs can get crowded, so it's best to plan ahead by checking the schedule at the Grand Canyon Visitor Center, Verkamp's Visitor Center, the activity desks at Bright Angel and Maswik Lodges, or online. On the North Rim, the North Rim Visitor Center next to the lodge posts the daily schedule. When you decide which programs to attend, find out from one of the rangers if they usually fill up and whether you need to sign up ahead of time.

DAY PROGRAMS
Every day the park offers many free ranger-guided hikes and nature walks, as well as lectures and discussions on the animals, human history, and geology of the canyon, at various spots around the park. The programs are most numerous and varied in the high seasons of spring, summer, and fall. In January and February rangers typically offer only two programs per day—one on canyon critters and another on the geology of Grand Canyon. To make up for this, the park offers several special "Cultural Demonstrator" programs (though not daily) in winter featuring Native American artists at the Desert View Watchtower.

NIGHT PROGRAMS
South Rim
Most nights during the summer there's a typically fascinating and free evening ranger program at the **McKee Amphitheater** if the weather's nice and the **Shrine of the Ages** if it isn't.

Night programs are generally not offered during January and February, ending after Christmas and beginning again during spring break in March. This varied program of lectures and night walks, on subjects ranging from astronomy to the Colorado River to "Surviving the Apocalypse at the Grand Canyon," is usually very popular, so it's best to plan ahead. For some of the most popular programs you must get a ticket to secure a spot, starting at 7:30pm at the Shrine of the Ages venue near Park Headquarters for an 8:30pm program at either venue. The amphitheater is behind and east of the Shrine of the Ages and can be reached via a spur from the Rim Trail, about 1.4 miles (2.3 km) east of the village.

North Rim

Night programs on the North Rim often involve stargazing, as the huge and clear sky above the sparsely populated plateau presents ideal conditions for the activity.

JUNIOR RANGERS

If you've got kids ages 4-12, before you start sightseeing, take them to the Grand Canyon Visitor Center and get them in the Junior Rangers program. The ranger will give them age-appropriate booklets, and throughout the day they'll earn a Junior Ranger badge and patch by fulfilling the fun and educational requirements, which include attending one of the ranger-led programs offered throughout the day.

ACCESSIBILITY

The **National Park Service's Access Pass** (888/467-2757; www.nps.gov), a free lifetime pass, grants admission for the pass-holder and three adults to all national parks, national forests, and the like, as well as discounts on interpretive services, camping fees, fishing licenses, and more. Apply in person at any federally managed park or wilderness area; you must show medical documentation of blindness or permanent disability.

Grand Canyon has many **accessible viewpoints,** and a large portion of the **Rim Trail,** the best vantage from which to see the canyon, is accessible to wheelchairs.

The park operates free shuttle bus service along the South Rim. All shuttle buses are wheelchair accessible (up to 30 in/76 cm wide and 48 in/122 cm long), with wheelchair ramps and low entrances and exits.

The National Park Service offers an **Accessibility Guide** for Grand Canyon National Park that outlines accessible facilities, services, and activities. It can be found at the park's visitor centers or downloaded from the park website (www.nps.gov/grca).

For advice and links to other helpful Internet resources, go to www.disabledtravelers.com, which is based in Arizona and is full of accessible travel information, though it's not specific to the state. For questions specific to Arizona, you may want to contact the state Department of Administration's **Office for Americans with Disabilities** (100 N. 15th Ave., Ste. 361, Phoenix; 602/542-6276 or 800/358-3617, TTY 602/542-6686).

TRAVELING WITH PETS

Throughout the park dogs must be kept on a leash at all times, and they are not allowed in buildings, on shuttle buses, or below the rim. **Yavapai Lodge** on the South Rim is the only in-park hotel that allows dogs, but there are several hotels in Williams and Flagstaff that are dog-friendly. The **South Rim Kennel,** next to Maswik Lodge, takes dogs and cats with proof of vaccinations, including for overnight boarding; reservations are highly recommended.

HEALTH AND SAFETY

EMERGENCY SERVICES

Dial 911 for emergencies. On the North Rim, where cell phone service is largely unavailable, there is a pay phone at the general store. In the inner canyon, there are emergency phones at the resthouses, developed campgrounds, ranger stations (Indian Garden and Phantom Ranch), and at the junction of the South Kaibab and Tonto Trails.

- **South Rim:** North Country HealthCare operates an **urgent care clinic and pharmacy** on the South Rim (1 Clinic Rd.; 928/638-2551; https://northcountryhealthcare.org; 9am-6pm daily Memorial Day-Labor Day, 8am-5pm daily Labor Day-Memorial Day). For after-hours emergencies dial 911.

- **North Rim:** The Kaibab Plateau and Grand Canyon National Park's North Rim have no emergency medical resources save for rangers. The closest hospital is 81 miles (130 km) away in Kanab, Utah, about a 1.5-hour drive. The closest emergency room is in Page, Arizona, 124 miles (200 km) away, a drive of about 2.5 hours.

- **Inner Canyon:** There are no hospitals or clinics inside the canyon, but there are regular ranger patrols below the rim on the Bright Angel, South Kaibab, and North Kaibab Trails, and at the ranger stations at Indian Garden on the Bright Angel Trail and Phantom Ranch.

EXTREME TEMPERATURES

The least of what the Arizona sun can do to you is not to be taken lightly. A **sunburn,** which comes on quicker than you'd think, can lead to skin cancer, and that can lead to death. If you get a sunburn, there's little you can do, save try to make yourself more comfortable. Stay out of the sun, of course, and try to keep cool and hydrated. There are dozens of over-the-counter balms available, but simple aloe works as well as anything. A popular home remedy is to gently dab the burned areas with vinegar. **Heat exhaustion** and **heatstroke** can affect anyone during the hot summer months, particularly during a long, strenuous hike in the sun. Common symptoms include nausea, lightheadedness, headache, or muscle cramps. **Dehydration** and loss of electrolytes are the common causes of heat exhaustion. The risks are even higher in the desert regions. If you or anyone in your group develops any of these symptoms, get out of the sun

CORONAVIRUS AND GRAND CANYON

At the time of writing in fall 2021, the coronavirus pandemic had significantly impacted the United States, including Grand Canyon and other areas covered in this guide. Most, if not all, destinations required that face masks be worn in enclosed spaces, but the situation was constantly evolving.

Now more than ever, Moon encourages its readers to be courteous and ethical in their travel. We ask travelers to be respectful to residents and mindful of the evolving situation in their chosen destination when planning their trip.

BEFORE YOU GO

- Check local websites (listed below) for updated **local restrictions** and the **overall health status** of destinations in this area.

- If you plan to fly, check with your airline as well as the **Centers for Disease Control and Prevention** (www.cdc.gov) for updated **recommendations** and **requirements.**

- Check the website of any museums and other venues you wish to patronize to confirm that they're open, if their hours have been adjusted, and to learn about any specific visitation requirements, such as **mandatory reservations** or **limited occupancy.**

immediately, stop all physical activity, and drink plenty of water. Heat exhaustion can be severe, and if untreated can lead to heatstroke, in which the body's core temperature reaches 105°F (40.5°C). Fainting, seizures, confusion, and rapid heartbeat and breathing can indicate the situation has moved beyond heat exhaustion.

Similar precautions hold true for **hypothermia,** which is caused by prolonged exposure to cold water or weather. This can happen on a canyon hike or backpacking trip without sufficient rain gear, or by staying too long in a cold body of water without a wetsuit. Symptoms include shivering, weak pulse, drowsiness, confusion, slurred speech, or stumbling. To treat hypothermia, immediately remove any wet clothing, cover the person with blankets, and feed him or her hot liquids.

ALTITUDE SICKNESS

Grand Canyon's South Rim sits at about 7,000 feet (2,134 m), its North Rim at 8,000 feet (2,438 m) and above, and some of the surrounding mountains reach 10,000 feet (3,048 m) or higher. Some of the mountain towns in the canyonlands sit between 5,000 feet (1,524 m) and 8,000 feet (2,438 m) above sea level. Lowlanders in relatively good shape may get headaches, a little dizziness, and shortness of breath while walking around Flagstaff and Grand Canyon, but very few will experience serious altitude sickness—the result of not getting enough oxygen, and therefore not enough blood flow to the brain. Still, take it easy in the higher elevations if you begin to feel tired and out of breath, dizzy, or euphoric. If you have heart or lung problems, you need to be more aware in the higher elevations.

- Pack **hand sanitizer,** a **thermometer,** and plenty of **face masks.** Consider packing **snacks, bottled water,** or even a **cooler** to limit the number of stops along your route.

- **Assess the risk** of entering crowded spaces, joining tours, and taking public transit.

- Expect **general disruptions.** Some park entrances and roads may be closed. Events may be postponed or cancelled. Some tours and venues may require reservations, enforce limits on the number of guests, be operating during different hours than the ones listed, or be closed entirely.

RESOURCES

- **National Park Service:** Grand Canyon National Park (www.nps.gov/grca), Glen Canyon National Recreation Area (www.nps.gov/glca)

- **U.S. Forest Service:** Southwestern Region (www.fs.usda.gov/r3)

- **State of Arizona:** Arizona Department of Health Services (www.azdhs.gov)

- **Native American Nations:** Havasupai (http://theofficialhavasupaitribe.com), Hopi (www.hopi-nsn.gov), Hualapai (http://hualapai-nsn.gov), Navajo (www.navajo-nsn.gov)

DANGEROUS ANIMALS

In this region, **poisonous rattlesnakes** and **scorpions** are a threat. When hiking or climbing in desert areas, never put your hand onto a ledge or into a hole that you can't see. Both are perfect lairs for snakes and scorpions. While snakebites are rarely fatal anymore, they're no fun either. If you are bitten, immobilize the affected area and seek immediate medical attention.

A scorpion's sting isn't as painful as you'd expect (it's about like a bee sting), and the venom is insufficient to cause any real harm. Still, it's not what you'd call pleasant, and experienced desert campers know to shake out their boots every morning, as scorpions and spiders are attracted to warm, moist, dark places.

Tarantulas and **black widow spiders** are present across much of the Colorado Plateau. Believe it or not, a tarantula's bite does not poison humans; the enzymes secreted when they bite turn the insides of frogs, lizards, and insects to a soft mush, allowing the tarantula to suck the guts from its prey. Black widow spiders, on the other hand, have a toxic bite. Although the bite is usually painless, it delivers a potent neurotoxin, which quickly causes pain, nausea, and vomiting. It is important to seek immediate treatment for a black widow bite; although few people actually die from these bites, recovery is helped along considerably by antivenin.

In the extremely rare case that you come into contact with a **mountain lion** (also called a cougar), stay calm. Do not run, do not bend down, do not approach the big cat; try to give it space to leave, but also attempt to make yourself seem bigger and more intimidating—raise your arms slowly, open your jacket, speak loudly. Odds are it will leave eventually, but if it continues to come at you, start throwing stones and sticks in its direction—but don't crouch or turn your back to pick them up. If you encounter a mountain lion on a trail, tell a ranger as soon as possible.

ILLNESS AND DISEASE

West Nile virus from mosquitoes and **hantavirus** from rodents are the long-shot threats to your health in this region, and both can be avoided by taking precautions. Use a DEET-based insect repellent to ward off mosquitoes and simply stay away from rodents. Hantavirus is an airborne infectious disease agent transmitted from rodents to humans when rodents shed hantavirus particles in their saliva, urine, and droppings and humans inhale the infected particles. It is easiest for a human to contract hantavirus in a contained environment, such as a cabin infested with mouse droppings, where the virus-infected particles are not thoroughly dispersed. Simply traveling to a place where the hantavirus is known to occur is not considered a risk factor. Camping, hiking, and other outdoor activities also pose low risk, especially if steps are taken to reduce rodent contact. The very first symptoms can occur anywhere between five days and three weeks after infection. They almost always include fever, fatigue, and aching muscles (usually in the back, shoulders, or thighs) and other flu-like conditions. Other early symptoms may include headaches, dizziness, chills, and abdominal discomfort (such as vomiting, nausea, or diarrhea). These are shortly followed by intense coughing and shortness of breath. If you have these symptoms, seek medical help immediately. Untreated infections of hantavirus are almost always fatal.

RESOURCES

GRAND CANYON

GRAND CANYON NATIONAL PARK
www.nps.gov/grca
The Grand Canyon's official website has extensive information on the park; go here for information about backcountry permits.

FEDERAL CAMPGROUND RESERVATIONS
www.recreation.gov
Use this site to make reservations at all federal parks, monuments, and national forests.

GRAND CANYON CONSERVANCY
www.grandcanyon.org
The main Grand Canyon nonprofit, Grand Canyon Conservancy publishes the best books about the canyon and operates the Field Institute, which offers guided backpacking and hiking trips, classes, and tours.

GRAND CANYON HIKERS AND BACKPACKERS ASSOCIATION
www.gchba.org
Find trail-level information and advice for your great Grand Canyon expedition.

PARK CONCESSIONAIRES

XANTERRA
www.grandcanyonlodges.com
Xanterra runs most of the hotels and eateries in Grand Canyon National Park, operates the historic Grand Canyon Railway, and offers bus tours and mule trips.

DELAWARE NORTH
www.visitgrandcanyon.com
This company operates Yavapai Lodge and its restaurants, the stores and delis at Market Plaza and Desert View, and Trailer Village.

ARIZONA TOURISM

ARIZONA OFFICE OF TOURISM
www.visitarizona.com
The official site for the state's office of tourism has basic information on the state's regions and lists various possible itineraries.

ROAD CONDITIONS

ARIZONA DEPARTMENT OF TRANSPORTATION
www.azdot.gov
For information about the conditions of Arizona's roadways.

INDEX

LIST OF MAPS

PHOTO CREDITS

National Parks Travel Guides from Moon

ACADIA
NATIONAL PARK
SEASIDE TOWNS · FALL FOLIAGE
CYCLING & PADDLING

HILARY NANGLE

ARCHES &
CANYONLANDS
NATIONAL PARKS
HIKING · BIKING
SCENIC DRIVES

JUDY JEWELL & W. C. MCRAE

BANFF
NATIONAL
PARK
HIKE · CAMP
SEE WILDLIFE

ANDREW HEMPSTEAD

CANADIAN
ROCKIES
WITH BANFF & JASPER NATIONAL PARKS
HIKE · CAMP
SEE WILDLIFE

ANDREW HEMPSTEAD

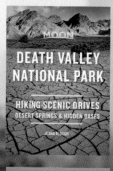

DEATH VALLEY
NATIONAL PARK
HIKING · SCENIC DRIVES
DESERT SPRINGS & HIDDEN OASES

JENNA BLOUGH

GLACIER
NATIONAL PARK
HIKING · CAMPING
LAKES & PEAKS

BECKY LOMAX

GRAND
CANYON
HIKE · CAMP
RAFT THE
COLORADO RIVER

TIM HULL

GREAT SMOKY
MOUNTAINS
NATIONAL PARK
HIKING · CAMPING
SCENIC DRIVES

JASON FRYE

JOSHUA TREE
& PALM SPRINGS
HIKING · SCENIC DRIVES
DESERT GETAWAYS

JENNA BLOUGH

ROCKY
MOUNTAIN
NATIONAL PARK
HIKE · CAMP
SEE WILDLIFE

ERIN ENGLISH

SEQUOIA &
KINGS CANYON
HIKING · CAMPING
WATERFALLS & BIG TREES

LEIGH BERNACCHI

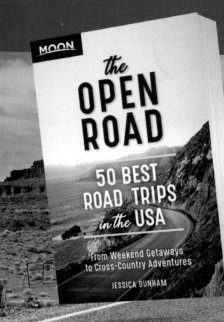

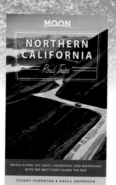

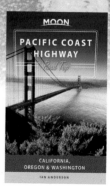

ROAD TRIP GUIDES FROM MOON

MOON
Pacific Crest Trail
PACIFIC CREST TRAIL

THE BEST TRAIL TOWNS, DAY HIKES, AND ROAD TRIPS IN BETWEEN

CAROLINE HINCHLIFF

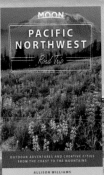

MOON
PACIFIC NORTHWEST
Road Trip

OUTDOOR ADVENTURES AND CREATIVE CITIES FROM THE COAST TO THE MOUNTAINS

ALLISON WILLIAMS

MOON
ROUTE 66
Road Trip

JESSICA DUNHAM

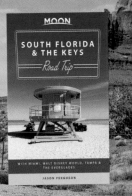

MOON
SOUTH FLORIDA & THE KEYS
Road Trip

WITH MIAMI, WALT DISNEY WORLD, TAMPA & THE EVERGLADES

JASON FERGUSON

MOON
SOUTHWEST
Road Trip

LAS VEGAS, ZION & BRYCE, MONUMENT VALLEY, SANTA FE & TAOS, AND THE GRAND CANYON

TIM HULL

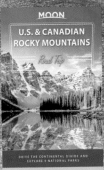

MOON
U.S. & CANADIAN ROCKY MOUNTAINS
Road Trip

DRIVE THE CONTINENTAL DIVIDE AND EXPLORE 9 NATIONAL PARKS

BECKY LOMAX

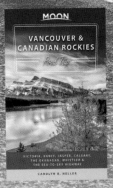

MOON
VANCOUVER & CANADIAN ROCKIES
Road Trip

VICTORIA, BANFF, JASPER, CALGARY, THE OKANAGAN, WHISTLER & THE SEA-TO-SKY HIGHWAY

CAROLYN B. HELLER

MOON
YELLOWSTONE TO GLACIER NATIONAL PARK
Road Trip

JACKSON HOLE, CODY, THE GRAND TETONS & THE ROCKY MOUNTAIN FRONT

CARTER G. WALKER

MOON
BASEBALL
Road Trips

TIMOTHY MALCOLM

THE COMPLETE GUIDE TO ALL THE BALLPARKS, WITH BEER, BITES, AND SIGHTS NEARBY

MOON
U.S. CIVIL RIGHTS TRAIL

A TRAVELER'S GUIDE TO THE PEOPLE, PLACES, AND EVENTS THAT MADE THE MOVEMENT

Deborah D. Douglas • Foreword by Bree Newsome Bass

Explore the US with expert authors like baseball writer Timothy Malcolm and journalist Deborah D. Douglas!

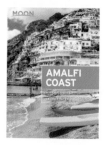
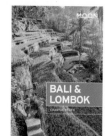

MAP SYMBOLS

═══	Highway	○	City/Town	🅿	Parking Area	🌲	Small Park
═══	Primary Road	◉	State Capital	🆃	Trailhead	▲	Mountain Peak
═══	Secondary Road	⊛	National Capital	🅱	Bike Trailhead		
= = =	Unpaved Road	★	Top 3 Sight	🅰	Camping	✛	Unique Natural Feature
- - - -	Trail	🚶	Top Hike	🅿	Picnic Area	✦	Unique Hydro Feature
───	Paved Trail	★	Highlight/Sight	Ⓜ	Mass Transit		
═══	Pedestrian Walkway	•	Accommodation	✕	Airport	🌊	Waterfall
········	Ferry	▼	Restaurant/Bar	✕	Airfield	⛷	Ski Area
-·-·-·	Railroad	■	Other Site	⛪	Place of Worship	◯	Glacier

CONVERSION TABLES

$°C = (°F - 32) / 1.8$
$°F = (°C \times 1.8) + 32$

1 inch = 2.54 centimeters (cm)
1 foot = 0.304 meters (m)
1 yard = 0.914 meters
1 mile = 1.6093 kilometers (km)
1 km = 0.6214 miles
1 fathom = 1.8288 m
1 chain = 20.1168 m
1 furlong = 201.168 m
1 acre = 0.4047 hectares
1 sq km = 100 hectares
1 sq mile = 2.59 square km
1 ounce = 28.35 grams
1 pound = 0.4536 kilograms
1 short ton = 0.90718 metric ton
1 short ton = 2,000 pounds
1 long ton = 1.016 metric tons
1 long ton = 2,240 pounds
1 metric ton = 1,000 kilograms
1 quart = 0.94635 liters
1 US gallon = 3.7854 liters
1 Imperial gallon = 4.5459 liters
1 nautical mile = 1.852 km

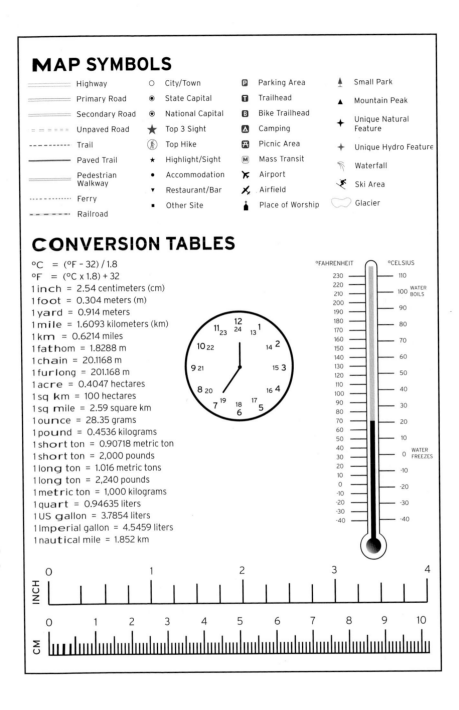

MOON BEST OF GRAND CANYON

Avalon Travel
Hachette Book Group
1700 Fourth Street
Berkeley, CA 94710, USA
www.moon.com

Editor: Nikki Ioakimedes
Managing Editor: Hannah Brezack
Copy Editor: Megan Anderluh
Production and Graphics Coordinator:
   Rue Flaherty
Cover Design: Marcie Lawrence
Interior Design: Tabitha Lahr
Map Editor: Albert Angulo
Cartographer: John Culp
Proofreader: Barbara Schultz

ISBN-13: 978-1-64049-678-1

Printing History
1st Edition — August 2022
5 4 3 2 1

Front cover photo: rafters in the
   Inner Gorge © Nicholas Motto |
   Dreamstime.com
Back cover photos: Hermit's Rest ©
   Maurizio De Mattei | Dreamstime.
   com (top), Indian Garden © Joshua
   Huang | Dreamstime.com (middle),
   South Rim view © Anna Dudko |
   Dreamstime.com (bottom)

Printed in Malaysia for Imago.